VENUS
GENIUS

THE FEMALE PRESCRIPTION
FOR INNOVATION

FABIENNE JACQUET

NEW DEGREE PRESS

VENUS GENIUS

The Female Prescription for Innovation

ISBN   978-1-63676-552-5 *Paperback*

          978-1-63676-124-4 *Kindle Ebook*

          978-1-63676-125-1 *Ebook*

VENUS GENIUS PRAISE

---

*Fabienne practices what she preaches and preaches what she is!
She incarnates the yin and the yang of innovation through her
personality, her experience and her sensitivities! Venus Genius
is a must read for anyone who must innovate to improve and
to simply move ahead; in other words for everyone!*

MARC SOMNOLET, CPG MARKETING EXECUTIVE,

ADJUNCT PROFESSOR AT NYU

*A compelling story of learning told by a scientist who has toiled
in R&D and business for more than 30 years, bringing creativity and innovation to organizations. If you get nothing
else (but you will) pay attention to Fabienne's brilliant point
about diversity and inclusion. Ask your diverse teams to dance
in order to see the benefits of diversity – both are the drivers
for future innovation*

STANLEY S. GRYSKIEWICZ, PH.D, FOUNDER & CHAIRMAN

EMERITUS, ASSOCIATION FOR MANAGERS OF INNOVATION

Fabienne Jacquet hits the nail on the head and shows us the formula to successful innovations. Venus Genius is packed with captivating stories, fascinating perspectives, and powerful data. It's an addictive and smart read for every male and female entrepreneur.

HANHLINH HOTRAN, AUTHOR OF SMART PATIENT

Loaded with numerous real world examples from a broad variety of people and perspectives, Venus Genius provides great insights, inspiration, and leadership into innovation for all! The many anecdotes and short stories draw the reader from page to page. It is both timely and timeless. An insightful read backed up by an entertaining and engaging personality with broad experience in innovation! Thank you Fabienne!

KIM TUTIN, SENIOR PROJECT MANAGER,

GEORGIA-PACIFIC CHEMICALS LLC

Venus Genius unleashes an exciting new outlook on the process of innovation, exploring the masculine and feminine sides of creativity. Delving into new strategies focusing on empathy and intuition, Jacquet leverages her extensive experience in leadership roles at Fortune 500 companies to tap into the rapidly growing female market. This fresh perspective helps to demystify innovation and makes a convincing case that feminine energy should be the driver for the future of innovation.

KARISSA Y. SANBONMUTSU, PRINCIPAL INVESTIGATOR

AT LOS ALAMOS NATIONAL LABORATORY

Fabienne Jacquet's 'Venus Genius' is a work of insightful feminine genius. The enjoyable and engaging style of writing, structure, flow, stories, personal stories, stats, research, references, inference, science, conclusions, speculations, aspirations, all work together brilliantly. Only Fabienne Jacquet could have produced this, a work of a lifetime.

JOE ROSS, CHIEF STRATEGY OFFICER, PRESENTATION

DIRECTOR, AND COACH AT IDEAS ON STAGE

New generation of girls need to know about Venus Genius philosophy and turn it into a key piece of their credentials. Girls need to know that there are others like Fabienne who have decided to step up and talk loudly about what is in their minds without waiting for someone's approval."

RAUL MALDONADO,

R&D MANAGER AT COLGATE PALMOLIVE

A refreshing look at innovation through an inquisitive, scientific, and feminine lens. A thoroughly addictive, learned, and fun read!

REBECCA WILLIAMS, FMCG INNOVATION

DELIVERY MANAGER

Fabienne is a much-needed voice in innovation. Her work raises awareness about the gender constructs that shape what is pursued, supported, and actualized in the business world. A must read for anyone looking to break free from limiting beliefs.

JEREMIE GLUCKMAN, MARKETER AND

AUTHOR IN THE SHADOW OF BIG TECH

In a sleek style, this book explains how human qualities, often reported to be more present in women, make the process of innovation more successful. A book that complements the socio-technical approach well and will enlighten practitioners of innovation.

ALAIN JACQUES, EXTERNAL INNOVATION-

EUROPE COLGATE PALMOLIVE - RETIRED

Venus Genius proposes a different way of looking at innovation, from both a masculine and feminine perspective. Jacquet's book tells us how we can improve the process of innovation by being aware of the lens we are comfortable with and acknowledging the need to innovate by "balancing both energies." This will be useful for anyone interested in innovation and entrepreneurship, and it will help educators to better prepare students to recognize the importance of incorporating masculine and feminine traits in the entrepreneurial process."

DEBORAH FINCH, ASSOCIATE TEACHING PROFESSOR

IN MARKETING, ENTREPRENEURSHIP & INNOVATION

AT THE UNIVERSITY OF MASSACHUSETTS

LOWELL, AUTHOR OF WAKE UP CALL

Fabienne Jacquet invites us to discover our inner "Venus Genius" as she deftly illustrates how traditionally under-valued traits are crucial to delivering game-changing inno-vation. You will enjoy her accessible style and light touch, and emerge with renewed energy to grow your innova-tion process.

CHERYL PERKINS, CEO OF INNOVATIONEDGE (BUSINESS WEEK TOP 25 INNOVATOR IN THE WORLD, CGT VISIONS LEADER AND STRATEGY THOUGHT LEADER)

Fabienne Jacquet, an amazing and inspiring expert in inno-vation has written an undeniable convincing statement. With her own energy, passion, fun and femininity she will take you on a journey that will substantiate the many reasons to level the feminine and masculine in innovation.

ANNETTE RAVEN, IT ANALYST & TEAMLEADER, NURSE

Fabienne's writings exemplify the power of gender diversity to innovation but at the core of her thesis it's a celebration of all the rich complexity that comes from all diversity. I'm blessed to know her as a friend and colleague and have great admiration for her work and contributions to inno-vation. This book will now introduce her to a world with-out boundaries.

TERENCE CALLOWAY - CHIEF PRODUCT SUPPLY OFFICER, ENERGIZER HOLDINGS, INC.

Venus Genius is a phenomenal book which provides new, fascinating ideas about the intersection between feminine and innovation. Fabienne's life perspectives are extraordinary, and captivating!

BARBARA EURIPIDES,

AUTHOR OF BRAINS, BEAUTY, BOSS

Fabienne unleashes a new perspective on the practice of innovation. Her book is insightful and well written. Game changing!!"

JORDAN PODOJIL,

AUTHOR OF THE FEMALE FOUNDING EDIT

*To my Mom Janine and my Dad André, for having allowed me
to be my authentic self, even if they didn't always approve!*

*To my brother Loïc, for his unconditional love
and support beyond our differences.*

To my husband Patrick, the sunshine of my life and my biggest fan.

CONTENTS

———

They didn't know it was impossible, so they did it.

MARK TWAIN

INTRODUCTION

———

Why should a sexual toy for women be shaped like a penis?

The answer to this is simple: The sex toy industry is a "boys' club," according to a *Fast Company* article.[1] Men are usually the ones designing the devices, so of course they assume that the only way for women to achieve pleasure is to mimic their wonderful organ.

It happens, though, that women have a clitoris, which has long been dismissed, demeaned, and misunderstood in the history of sexual anatomy. I am sorry to report that when a French physician dissected this organ for the first time in 1545, he named it *membre honteux*—"the shameful appendage"— and declared its sole purpose to be urination, according to a *Scientific American* article. That article reports another fun fact for men who are obsessed with size and consider the clitoris an atrophied penis: *"It is not just some pea-sized nub. Around 90 percent of the clitoris' bulk lies beneath the surface,*

———

1   Diana Budds, "The Female Engineers Building Better Sex Toys," *Fast Company,* March 31, 2017.

*with arms that flare out up to nine centimeters into the pelvis.
And by the way, it is boasted [to have] two to three times as
many nerve endings as the penis."* [2]

Understanding this sheds a totally different light on how
the female orgasm works, driven by the clitoris and not the
vagina as stated by Sigmund Freud.

Women's sexual pleasure is still a taboo subject—with a long
road ahead. Despite their courageous attempts at addressing this market, women still face patriarchal barriers. Lora
diCarlo's Osé massager was granted a CES 2019 Innovation
Award in robotics prior to the CES (Consumer Electronics
Show) by a panel of independent expert judges for its cut-
ting-edge technology. However, the CTA (Consumer Technology Association) revoked the award a month later, citing
the product as "immoral."[3]

In Lindsay Goldwert's SPENT podcast, Alexandra Fine, who
has a master's in clinical psychology, takes us through her
journey. She cofounded the company Dame Products with
Janet Lieberman (an MIT engineer), which manufactures
innovative sexual wellness toys. They had to overcome a lot
of barriers and Alexandra struggled for her business to be
taken seriously and to make it known: advertising is allowed
for erectile dysfunction, but it is a challenge for women's
sexual pleasure.

---

2   Rachel E. Gross, "The Clitoris, Uncovered: An Intimate History," *Scien-
     tific American,* March 4, 2020.

3   Natashah Hitti, "Ces Restores Lora Dicarlo's Sex Toy Award After Sexism
     Outcry," *Dezeen,* May 13, 2019.

Money and sex are running the world and control relationships, but women are ashamed of talking about both and/or made to feel it is morally wrong to have those conversations.[4]

It was also difficult for Janet as a female engineer in this male-dominated industry. It took all their passion for sexual health and a great deal of empathy for the female experience to make this company successful.

Before we go any further, I want to make a key statement: This book is not about women versus men; it is not even about gender. It is about celebrating the duality of the feminine and the masculine in all human beings and making sure we activate both energies to create innovation that brings true value to our world.

It just happens that in general, due to biological and cultural influences, women tend to have a stronger feminine side and men a stronger masculine side, and that the world has been mainly driven by masculine energy. There is a trend in rebalancing those differences with gender fluidity, but as of today, we cannot just ignore gender; this is our history and our society. As a scientist, I cannot discard facts; this is why I will have to make gendered statements and advocate for gender equality in innovation.

Part 1 of this book is aimed at demystifying innovation, its process, and the respective roles of the genders. It shows how it's been very masculine until now, depriving us of

---

4   Alexandra Fine, "Sex & Money," December 15, 2019, in *SPENT*, produced by Lindsay Goldwert, Apple podcast, MP3 audio, 53:22.

the emotional feminine energy that is the actual engine for meaningful innovation.

In Part 2, we will detail the $20+ trillion business opportunity of the female market, how women have natural advantages to address it, and how feminine energy should be the driver for the future of innovation.

Plenty of evidence demonstrates that innovation is a catalyst for growth in any business. The scope of innovation has evolved over time. During the Industrial Revolution, innovation focused on science and the invention of new machines and products. Its productivity was measured through patents. This explains in part why women were kept outside of the innovation arena, as science was not considered to be a suitable profession for women.

Economists like Joseph Schumpeter pushed the innovation concept toward business, outlining the difference between "invention" and "innovation": innovation brings invention to market.[5] Innovation took off in the 1980s in the business world, leading to "Most Innovative Company" rankings and a flurry of innovation conferences.

Unfortunately, the evolution of innovation to include business didn't lead to gender equality. According to the Equality of Opportunity Project, the gender gap in innovation is shrinking gradually over time, but at the current rate, it will take another 118 years to reach gender parity. That's a shame.

---

5   Emma Green, "Innovation: The History of a Buzzword," *The Atlantic*, June 13, 2013.

If women and minorities were to invent at the same rate as white men with high incomes (top 20 percent), the rate of innovation in America would quadruple.[6]

Given that the Equality of Opportunity Project's research has found that innovation ability does not vary substantially across all groups, this result implies that many "lost Einsteins" exist among the underrepresented groups: people who would have had high-impact inventions had they had the opportunity to become inventors. Many of those people are women: if girls were as exposed to female inventors as boys are to male inventors, the gender gap in innovation would fall by half.[7]

We therefore have a backlog of great innovators with women. It has been proven that women are great inventors and creators according to history, although most are not recognized as such. Did you know that Grace Hopper invented the compiler that translated written language into computer code and designed Harvard's Mark I computer, a five-ton, room-size machine, in 1944?[8]

---

6   Alex Bell, Raj Chetty, Xavier Jaravel, Neviana Petkova, and John Van Reenen, *Who Becomes an Inventor in America? The Importance of Exposure to Innovation*, 2018, from the Equality of Opportunity Project, team led by Stanford economist Raj Chetty. 1; 5.

7   Ibid., 4.

8   Melina Glusac, "14 World-Changing Innovations by Women That Were Originally Credited to Men," *Insider*, Mar 8, 2020.

While giving women a larger role in innovation would be just and fair, even more importantly, it would inspire younger women and give them the confidence that they can innovate.

I could witness in my career that women are equipped with the appropriate skills for innovation.

Research from *Harvard Business Review* shows that for companies tasked with understanding female consumers (74 percent of companies target women), leveraging women innovators improves the likelihood of their success by 144 percent.[9] Another study from MIT and Carnegie Mellon proved that while increasing diversity in general increases performance, there is also evidence that women specifically have a major impact. In fact, they not only found that teams that included women earned better results at problem solving, but that the higher the proportion of women was, the better the teams did.[10]

This brings us to a bigger question: why does innovation often fail, especially when it comes to innovating for women?

9   Sylvia Ann Hewlett, Melinda Marshall, and Laura Sherbin, "How Women Drive Innovation and Growth," *Harvard Business Review,* August 23, 2013.

10   Derek Thompson, "The Secret to Smart Groups: It's Women," *The Atlantic,* January 18, 2015.

THERE ARE A LOT OF MISCONCEPTIONS ABOUT INNOVATION

- Innovation has to be managed like a business (driven by the masculine priorities of effectiveness, performance, KPIs (Key Performance Indicators), etc.).
- Innovation is reserved for the elite.
- Innovation is driven by processes.
- Emotions have no place in business; they don't produce money.
- The female market is a "niche" market, and women are happy with the products and services developed for them.

Based on my research, interviewing, and experience, it seems that this represents a very narrow view of innovation and limits its potential. Rebalancing innovation from the rational toward the emotional—and the masculine toward the feminine—can only benefit its outcome:

- Some feminine traits, like empathy or intuition, are absolutely critical to develop meaningful and sustainable innovation: we need a mix of traditionally masculine and feminine traits for successful innovation.
- Anybody can be an innovator if they have the right mindset and practice the right skills; moreover, given our brain plasticity, anybody can acquire so-called "masculine" or "feminine" skills.
- True innovation is driven by human creativity.
- Emotions make the difference between an innovation that connects to consumers and one that doesn't. Emotional connections bring value, hence increasing the bottom line.

- The female market is a $20+ trillion opportunity, and it is totally underserved.

Innovation has been my career and life DNA. I have always been very curious, and as a rebel, I am always challenging the status quo to try to improve the way things are. Having been brought up between two brothers and having studied as a scientist, I learned to function from my masculine side. Only later in life did I reconnect with my feminine energy. I experienced firsthand how incorporating my femininity grounded me and improved not only my personal life, but also my performance at work. I spent more than thirty years innovating in the corporate world, first as a scientist and then as a marketer and business developer. I explored all types of innovation: fundamental, short-term, long-term, strategic, and open innovation, in categories primarily targeting women.

Marrying my masculine-structured approach and my feminine instincts helped me establish a proven track record of successful innovation. I didn't lose the power of masculine traits like being logical, focused, action orientated, and assertive, which are necessary for an innovation to hit the market. I complemented those skills with intuition, collaboration, and nurturing, a feminine energy that allowed me to create and develop the best ideas to be further brought to the commercial level.

Then came my *AHA!* moment. At that time, I was working in technology in a corporate environment. My team was trying to develop a shower gel that would rate high on emotional connection with consumers. It was a tough challenge, as a shower gel is merely a commodity product to which consumers don't develop a strong attachment. All the prototypes we developed rated high on functional benefits like lathering, cleansing, and even pleasant scent, but they did not achieve the mark for emotional benefits. We had applied a consumer testing methodology that evaluated the emotional impact of the product: consumers rated prototypes by identifying a facial expression or visual representing specific emotions like joy, disgust, freedom, or stress. All our prototypes rated very low. The team was quite down.

Soon after, I attended an intercompany brainstorming "hoo-ha" session organized by a partner expert in sensory evaluation: Eurosyn. The objective of the workshop was to try to understand how to create emotional and multisensorial products and services. The guest speaker, the artist Polar, started to sing. The song was about losing love because of a lack of communication and understanding. At the end we all had tears in our eyes, which felt awkward in this business environment. We asked him: *"How is it that you created something that we were able to feel so deeply?"* He looked at us and said: *"Well, because I created that song with my emotions; I put all my emotions in it."*

And suddenly it hit me: in the corporate world, we are trying to create the perfect functional product with all the appropriate features it should have. And then at the end, when it's ready, we say: *"Hey, now let's connect with the consumers and put some emotions into it with advertising."* But it doesn't work like that.

Back at the office, I put a small multifunctional team together. The first volunteers to join were women, which is interesting to note. We talked about the emotions we wanted to spark in consumers: guilty pleasure, freedom, abandonment, sense of space. Then we spent full days all together to cocreate prototypes with external experts and consumers. We started from the emotions we could feel when showering, making sure that all sensorial elements were supporting that emotion. The winning prototype received the highest emotional scores of the category in the test we had previously failed. The imagery was a Tuscany-inspired scene with vineyards: the rich texture evoked luxury, the color was a profound burgundy, and the smell was very gourmand. Needless to say, we celebrated.

A lesson is that if you don't create something starting with your emotions and your heart, it doesn't connect emotionally with consumers. This is especially important for the female market. When basic needs like performance and convenience are met, the emotional connection makes the difference in the purchase decision.

FEMININE ENERGY BRINGS INNOVATION TO ANOTHER LEVEL

In this book, I feel the need to share this knowledge and propose a new innovation framework.

In her book *Wolfpack,* Abby Wambach tells a beautiful story about wolves: when wolves return to a certain location, they are the savers of nature and the ecosystem. Abby says that women now are the savers and are here for salvation. It's our time, driven by the heart, not the ego. In this book, I am extending this metaphor to innovation and presenting a new framework for innovators based on feminine wisdom to address the weaknesses of the current system.[11]

After all, feminism did a pretty good job of showing that women can do what men do. What we haven't achieved is showing that men can do what women do.

JESSAMYN NEUHAUS.[12]

I have tapped into my thirty+ years of innovation experience in the corporate world and have conducted significant research and professional interviews to identify the feminine traits that are most critical for successful innovation. We will explore in the book how, regardless of gender, any human being possesses those latent feminine traits. Due to biological and social-cultural factors, most women develop them more than men, which makes them especially suited for innovation.

I came up with a "feminine success formula" for innovation—hey, I am a chemist—that I will reveal in Chapter 8 of this book. Part 3 will review in detail the six feminine traits I have selected: empathy, nurturing, inclusivity, intuition, gratitude, and collaboration, and how they contribute to sustainable innovation.

---

11   *Shona Project*, "Abby Wambach: Be the Wolf," July 5, 2018, video, 4:59.

12   Jessica Contrera, "The End Of 'Shrink It and Pink It': A History Of Advertisers Missing the Mark with Women," *The Washington Post*," June 9, 2016.

There will be a "Let's Practice" section focused on tips that help individuals become better at honing each feminine trait. Indeed, as we are dealing with "soft" and not "hard" skills, it is a long practice that needs to be integrated into one's life. The objective is to prepare individuals for further practice applied to business and teams.

Part 4 will describe the "feminine success formula" in action.

This book is meant to be useful to anybody who is curious about innovation and wants to tackle it under a different angle, regardless of their gender. You can be an innovator in a big company who wants to make a difference, a startup who doesn't know where to start with innovation, or an HR employee who needs to retain talents by empowering and motivating them. It is especially suited to any company (small or big) that sells products targeted to women and wants to reach them more efficiently.

I hope you'll enjoy this journey exploring the world of innovation through a feminine lens, the mysteries of the masculine and feminine brains—if such entities exist—some juicy anecdotes of women's daily lives in a world designed by men, and, to finish, a description of the feminine innovation framework: how to unlock your feminine traits and create meaningful and sustainable innovation, wherever you stand on the masculine-feminine continuum.

1

HOW WE
GOT HERE

1

DEMYSTIFYING INNOVATION

———

Innovation is the action or process of innovating.

Wow! Google's featured definition is definitely very helpful, isn't it?[13]

"What is innovation?" is the million-dollar question. In fact, it is an almost two-trillion-dollar question, which is roughly the number of hits one gets when searching for "innovation definition." Recently, innovation has become a buzzword that a lot of people use without really knowing what it is and understanding what it covers.

SO, WHAT'S INNOVATION?

In my transition from corporate to the world of entrepreneurs and small businesses, I realized that people considered

———

13   "Google: Innovation definition," landing page, accessed September 9, 2020.

innovation as reserved for the elite. Most of them did not really understand what innovation was. Even big companies can be overwhelmed by innovation. A June 2020 report from BCG (Boston Consulting Group) reveals that 25 percent of big companies are confused by innovation, with inconsistent commitment and resource investment.[14]

Very smart innovators and experts went through the exercise of defining innovation. The outcome can be complicated or pompous. I personally gravitate around the short and impactful ones, like: *"Innovation is creativity that ships,"* (Steve Jobs) or *"The future delivered"* (Jorge Barba).[15]

Still, innovation can sound sophisticated and intimidating.

I would argue that it should be accessible and that anyone can be an innovator if one is curious, passionate, courageous, and ready to develop the right skills.

People pigeonhole creativity as belonging to a single individual or group of geniuses; they don't realize that every human has this incredible capacity to imagine and to change things.
ANTHROPOLOGIST AUGUSTIN FUENTES.[16]

---

14   Michael Ringel, Ramón Baeza, Rahool Panandiker, and Johann D. Harnoss, "Successful Innovators Walk the Talk—The Most Innovative Companies 2020," *BCG,* June 22, 2020.

15   Idea to Value, "What is innovation? 15 innovation experts give us their definition," home page, accessed August 23, 2020.

16   Ryan Leveille, ""Hybrid Thinking" Leaders Will Prosper: Part 2—Humans Were Born to Create at Every Age," *Medium,* Feb 18, 2019.

For my own definition, I opted for very simple language:

Something new that creates value.

"SOMETHING NEW THAT CREATES VALUE"
When we think about innovation, we usually think product innovation (be it a beauty cream or a car), or technology (digital technologies, patents). Innovation is much broader. It can be a service (new distribution system like takeout or online selling), a process (Henry Ford's invention of the world's first moving assembly line), or a system (e.g. creating the first health savings account). It can also be an undiscovered combination of existing elements into a new breakthrough (the iPhone). What we more often see these days is business model innovation, like the "platform" business of Uber or Airbnb.

"SOMETHING NEW THAT CREATES VALUE"
If what you create is not new, it cannot be innovation. Now, it's all relative depending on the scope and impact of the innovation. It can be new to the world (the vaccine concept), or new to the industry (the electric car). Copying an innovation to apply it to your own company is not innovating. However, as we saw with the iPhone, combining existing technologies or innovations into a new concept or business model is innovation.

For instance, launching a shower gel with a new fragrance, which will basically cannibalize existing business, is not innovative. Launching a shower gel variant that emotionally connects to consumers to the point that it becomes viral on social media and brings incremental business by attracting new users and non-category users is somewhat innovative.

If we look at the etymology, innovation was introduced in the 1540s, from the Latin *innovatus*, past participle of *innovare*: "to renew, restore." It also means transforming into something new, giving a new life to something.[17] We may think of artists like the French painter Blase, who transforms classical paintings by adding a contemporary element.[18]

In our interview, Nelida Quintero, an architect and environmental psychologist, reminded us to stay humble: *"I feel that sometimes we push too hard for being original: be the first or be new. But innovation, from my perspective, often happens when redesigning, rethinking, reconsidering something within different contexts or from different standpoints, and that in itself could be innovative."*

There is therefore an entire spectrum of newness, from minor to world-changing.

"SOMETHING NEW THAT CREATES **VALUE**"
This is the most important component of the innovation equation. When we think value, we first think "green:"

---

17   *Online Etymology Dictionary*, s.v. "innovate," accessed August 23, 2020.

18   Vanida DL, "French Artist Restores Flea Market Paintings and Adds His Own Stories to Them," *Boredpanda*, posted 4 years ago, accessed August 23, 2020.

bottom line, money. It's certainly important, but value is far more than that. Like beauty, it's in the eye of the beholder.

It reminds me of a great training I had in the corporate world around partnerships given by the Rhythm of Business consultancy. When talking about collaborations, they made us think about the value we could bring to the other party. They called it "currencies." Beyond revenues, it could be image, connections, credibility, or knowledge. It depends on what you need the most in your current situation. It's well known that if you are lost in Death Valley, a bottle of water is of better value than a $500 bill.

To summarize, as a simple example of all words being used, imagine this: a young entrepreneur created a rock-climbing training. One might argue that this is not an innovation. Well, when you know it was for abused women, suddenly it sounds like innovation: *something* (a rock climbing training), *new* (dedicated to abused women; this didn't exist before) that creates *value* (bringing back confidence, self-esteem, and pride to women and therefore changing their lives).

Anne Hoag, director and associate professor at State College, Pennsylvania, and fellow author, shared a story that is required to appropriately set the scene:

"I was a young professional in Chicago working for a big advertising agency at the entry level; this is the early 1980s. I was looking for some kind of hobby, something that I could afford. There was a knitting shop in my neighborhood, and I thought maybe I would like to try it, as I didn't know how to knit. So, I

walked into the shop, and I asked: is there a way I could learn how to knit? And there was this woman."

Here I'd like to pause so that we can all enjoy how Anne describes the woman:

"So it was just a yarn store. You walked in and there was a table in the middle, and this woman who later introduced herself as 'Sis.' She was an older lady with a cigarette dangling out of her mouth; as she's knitting, ashes would fall on the yarn. I asked if there was a way I could learn how to knit. She was very gruff and not particularly friendly. She said: 'Yeah, you just buy your yarn and needles from me and I'll teach you how to knit.' And I said, 'All right, I'll do that, I can actually make a scarf.' She got really annoyed and said: 'No, that's not how we do it. Your first thing should be something you really, really want to wear. Go home, find a picture and bring it back to me; don't come back till you find something you really like.'

"And so I did, I went through whatever magazines and found back that Chanel jacket I loved. I'm twenty-three years old and starting to work. There's no way I can afford a Chanel jacket."

You'll tell me: nothing innovative or feminine here. Hang on.

"Back to the store, Sis looked at the picture and told me: 'Yeah, you can make that.' And then she walked around the smoky shop and showed me the yarns and the needles and just wrote the pattern on the spot. All along, she was very gruff, like, 'Buy this, do this. Here, sit down here.' And then she starts showing me. There was a lot of trial and error. I had to keep coming back to the shop and having her show me what to do.

"This is when I discovered what her model was: she had eve-
nings where you could come and sit in the shop with other
women. I bought more yarn from her, and eventually, I did
end up making the jacket. First thing I ever did. I've never knit
anything before, and the first thing I made was a first-grade
knockoff of a Chanel jacket.

"That was clearly her way of doing business: it was not about
knitting; she created kind of a community. That was the early
1980s and I don't know of any other business like that at that
time. The community was the customer, but it was also the
product, in the same way that every internet business has
been ever since."

Does it sound a little bit more like innovation now? Let's
decrypt it, starting with the definition: *something* (a knitting
shop that doubles as a workshop) *new* (the combination of
a product and a community-based service was a new business model at that time) that creates *value* (allowing a young
woman to proudly learn a new skill while having access to a
belonging she could never afford).

This story is actually very rich with beautiful things to learn
about innovation.

- A classical learning process would call for doing something easy first: knit a scarf. It is a quite innovative
  approach to say: No, follow your heart and passion
  instead; knit something you will just love! Start from
  emotions, not logic.
- Anne's description of Sis doesn't give a very feminine
  image. However, in her approach, Sis displayed some

key feminine traits that we will detail later on in this book:

- Empathy for a young girl who couldn't afford a Chanel jacket
- Nurturing that relationship by patiently teaching her how to knit that jacket
- Intuition of the new model of a "conscious" business: bringing social and emotional impact while growing the bottom line
- Collaboration by creating this community of women supporting one another in their creative journey.
- It also poses the question: what's feminine? We will cover this question in the next chapter.

WHAT ABOUT THE INNOVATION PROCESS?

Searching "innovation process" in Google brings roughly the same number of hits as "innovation definition." Most of the descriptions are very extensive and complicated, including loops, numerous decision points, and steps.

If you are an innovation leader in a big corporation, you certainly have seen those consultants' charts with beautifully drawn processes that end up collecting dust in office drawers.

I am not saying we don't need processes for innovation. We do need the rigor and structure. Trying to simplify and demystify innovation does not mean it is easy. Some people picture innovation as cool people with crazy hair having fun in a room full of bean bags. But innovating is very challenging: it's "blood, sweat, and tears."

Processes are necessary; they just need to find their place at the right time, and they cannot lead to meaningful innovation without human creativity.

I propose an oversimplified process. In reality, it's not linear and includes numerous iterations. This is to fit the purpose of understanding the human traits associated with each step.

The process is composed of two phases. The *front-end* (or discovery phase), and the *back-end* (or execution phase).

The *front-end* of innovation goes from "nothing" to a prototype. The *back-end* develops, validates and scales up the prototype to finally launch a commercial product. Let's specify the notion of prototype as definitions vary. A prototype can be physical or virtual, as long as it proves the technical, financial, and legal feasibility of the idea. Its execution must include technical specifications, deliver the claimed consumer benefits, and describe the business model. It should also be scalable.

As an example, when we developed our relaxing shower gel prototype, it was a physical sample. All ingredients were approved by safety; the formula backbone was proprietary to the company and had been used for years in manufacturing. As it had been cocreated with consumers, we knew it delivered the emotional benefit of relaxation. It would be distributed through the company's traditional channels.

The *back-end* of the process requires focus, rigor, action-oriented tasks, quick decision-making, logical planning, and setting goals and boundaries. Those traits are considered as typically masculine. I will not elaborate in this book as this part of the process is not its focus.

The *front-end* of innovation, on the other hand, calls on our feminine traits. Being emotional, nurturing, supportive, intuitive, accepting, empathetic, and relational is absolutely key to successfully perform the front-end actions:

- Understand: the consumer, market, environment, and key stakeholders
- Ideate: from the gathered information, brainstorm ideas, and connect the dots
- Screen: the ideas to identify those with the best potential
- Prototype: develop a physical or virtual representation of the selected idea(s)

In Part 3 of the book, we will review in detail the six specific feminine traits that I identified for the front-end, based on my years of innovation experience in the corporate world as well as on significant research.

WHAT DOES IT TAKE TO BE AN INNOVATOR?

Looking at the entire innovation process, it becomes quite evident that being an innovator requires a quite balanced profile. According to professor of psychology and management Mihaly Csikszentmihalyi, in short, an ideal innovator profile should include traits that may sound contradictory: be both extraverted and introverted, rebellious and conservative, or alternate between fantasy and a rooted sense of reality.[19]

When I am asked to introduce myself, I often joke that "I am half French, half American, half scientist, and half marketer." Yes, I know, too many halves, but as we say in French: "When you love, you don't count!"

Maybe this is why I was destined to be an innovator.

We have to admit that it's quite a challenge to find all those traits in one person. The good news is that we all have a natural duality in ourselves that we can leverage: the masculine/ feminine.

Here's a very interesting finding:

When tests of masculinity and femininity are given to young people, over and over one finds that creative and talented girls are more dominant and tough than other girls, and creative boys are more sensitive and less aggressive than their male peers.[20]

This is the perfect proof that innovators need a balance between their masculine and feminine sides.

In the previous shower gel example, I tapped into my feminine energy to identify the right emotions, but I had to rely

---

19   Faisal Hoque, "10 Paradoxical Traits Of Creative People," *Fast Company,* September 4, 2013.

20   Ibid.

on my masculine rigor and organization to develop the actual prototype.

DO MEN AND WOMEN INNOVATE THE SAME WAY?

There is a fundamental difference in the approach to innovation by men and women.

During our interview, Maiko Kyogoku, owner of Bessou and one of the rare female restaurant owners in New York City, made this revealing statement:

I noticed that men are problem fixers. They see an issue and they need to find a solution right away. There is a certain rigidity in that type of thinking when you always have to be the fixer. In my personal experience, I [as a woman] let my intuition guide me, as there isn't a clear answer or fix for everything or pressure to do it. It's kind of a sixth sense, a flexibility that helped me make something that has never been done before.

Andrea Simon, corporate anthropologist and author of *On The Brink: A Fresh Lens to Take Your Business to New Heights,* confirmed that in a lot of companies, she had to help men innovate: "*The way the brain works is it takes the facts and creates a story around it. Most men only saw the things that fit it and deleted everything that didn't fit. We had to help them innovate by seeing things through a fresh lens.*"

My friend Joe Ross, chief strategy officer, presentation director, and business and personal coach at Ideas on Stage, has worked with a lot of executives on their presentations. He noticed that for innovation, "*The masculine approach is all about 'reduction:' okay, there's a problem. I'm going to try to look for a solution. And I'm going to reduce it down to the one or two components, and I'm going to try to control it and manipulate it. And at the end, if it doesn't produce a good solution, I'm just going to hammer until it works. And of course, it doesn't. You know, that's absolutely the inverse of creativity. Creativity is about being open. It's about being able to explore and accept and letting the happy accidents in serendipity. So, I think you're spot on."*

This masculine attitude of problem solving can be totally right. We all enjoy it in our daily lives. It also has its place in innovation for incremental growth.

When you're looking for more breakthrough innovation, you need to activate other skills. You need to get comfortable with uncertainty, take the time to reflect, listen to your emotions, and be extremely persistent, as failure is an inherent part of innovation. You need to put yourself at risk and be okay with losing control.

Stay hungry, stay foolish.

STEVE JOBS[21]

Raj Sisodia is a thought leader of the Conscious Capitalism movement, the FW Olin Distinguished Professor of

---

21 Stanford News, "'You've got to find what you love,' Jobs says," *Stanford*, June 12, 2005.

Global Business at Babson College, and the coauthor of *Shakti Leadership: Embracing Feminine and Masculine Power in Business.*

During our interview, he outlined some differences in the way men and women consider innovation:

"I think that the masculine ideal [of innovation] is more kind of the 'lone genius' working away in a basement or a garage, or maybe two people, a buddy. As for women, I think the wisdom of the group is what propels innovation . . . as well as a greater sensitivity to inclusivity."

This may reflect that the masculine is more into scarcity and competition, while the feminine is more about abundance and cooperation, as we'll see in the next chapter.

Raj confirms what I had identified in my experience: In my more masculine phase, I was a lone wolf during my PhD. When I embraced my feminine energy, I was more open to collaboration for a new type of innovation, which certainly prompted me to move to marketing.

Raj also brought a new, intriguing angle:

The other thing that I think happens is this idea of trade-offs. I think men are more accustomed to thinking of win, lose, and trade-off. So, like with food, it can either be nutritious or it can be delicious. Well, we need both. We don't have to sacrifice one for the other. But it takes creativity to break the trade-off, and I sense that women might be intuitively better at it.

My friend Lisa Lipkin is the founder of *Storystrategies* and has a wonderful career in storytelling. She shared the disappointment her mother felt when she went to the hospital to get her regular chemo treatment for blood cancer. They recently renovated the hospital:

"It used to be everybody sitting in one big group together, and she loved that she could talk to all the other patients and hear their stories and get tips; it was really comforting for her because the sessions can last hours.

"Anyway, they renovated, and they made private cubicles, and now she has nobody to talk to. And that was their idea of making it nicer. I couldn't help but wonder who decided that was a better medical treatment? It smacked of money. Someone on the board must have assumed rich people don't want to associate with the hoi polloi. But it also felt like a classic Western medical decision too, one that always puts emotional connection second to other technical factors. I thought it was a perfect example of not considering the emotional cost and benefits: not realizing that part of healing is hearing the stories of others and being connected to others."

This is a good example of a "trade-off" change that seems mostly based on practical and monetary considerations without spending too much time on the emotional aspect. Or at least it was perceived as such by my friend Lisa, even if they had the best intentions with the remodeling. Maybe keeping a smaller common room while offering some private booths would have avoided the trade-off.

IT TAKES BOTH THE MASCULINE AND
THE FEMININE TO INNOVATE

John Downer is a talent acquisition leader and HR expert I had the pleasure to work with in my corporate life. When discussed the topic of both the masculine and the feminine being needed for innovation, he rightly pointed out that it was part of a *"Larger movement that requires a different type of unity amongst women and men. I think it needs to transcend industries; it needs to transcend business lines."*

Crises like the COVID-19 pandemic are opportunities to see the best and the worst in human beings and to outline the differences between the masculine and the feminine. Some people follow their masculine energy and compete without collaboration to try to get first to the miracle solution (e.g. a vaccine), pursuing fame and money. Some others—women and men—follow their feminine energy to heal those who suffer.

Now, if we combine the masculine and the feminine to globally collaborate at creating a vaccine and kindly making it available to all people in the world, this will make a difference.

Kim Tutin had roles including technology scout and senior project manager at Georgia-Pacific Chemicals LLC. She has a terrific thirty-four-year technical career in that company. As I listened to her talk about innovation, it appeared to me that she was a great example of embracing the duality of both masculine and feminine traits for successful innovation. She defined an innovator as *"someone that's creative, likes to solve problems, is willing to push the envelope, and wants to make an impact on society to hopefully make the world a better place."*

I could feel all her passion for innovation when she talked about a project she was leading: *"What's so exciting about this particular project is that it's good for the industry with an amazing unique technology, and it's also good for the world because it reduces greenhouse gas emissions, so it's a very, very rare project."*

She looked to me like a perfectly balanced innovator who enjoyed the rational and logical side of the technology while appreciating the more emotional side of doing something good for the environment.

'✱✱✱'

We've explored:

- The definition of innovation and its processes
- How anyone who is passionate and develops the right skills can innovate
- That both masculine and feminine traits are essential for successful innovation
- How feminine traits like empathy, nurturing, intuition, or collaboration are critical to the discovery part of the process.

Let's go deeper now into the feminine and the masculine.

I want to reiterate that this book is not about opposing women and men. Its purpose is to report facts, better understand what the feminine and masculine can bring to innovation, and make sure we balance both energies to create better innovation for the world.

2

IS INNOVATION GENDERED?

———

My company INNOVEVE® is about innovation through the feminine lens, leveraging feminine traits like empathy, nurturing, and intuition. I was pitching my FEMimicry® workshop to a company that provides training to CEOs. As their members are almost exclusively men, I could feel the tension building up in the room as I was going through the feminine traits of my success formula and describing the exercises the participants would do.

I could see the body language of the people in the room who were physically withdrawing or nervously shifting on their seats at the sound of the words "empathy," "intuition," "nurturing," or simply "feminine." I could even perceive the discomfort of the remote attendees just by looking at their facial expressions on the screen. At one point, one of the men said: *"I don't really buy into your idea that feminine traits are necessary in innovation. Steve Jobs was an exceptional innovator, and he had nothing feminine."*

I breathed before calmly answering: *"Well, actually in the workshop, I give Steve Jobs as the perfect example of a feminine trait that's indispensable for meaningful innovation: intuition."*

IS CREATIVITY FEMININE OR MASCULINE?

My theory is that the feminine is more appropriate at the beginning of the innovation process, and the masculine is more appropriate at the end, as the front-end of innovation (discovery phase) is unknown and chaotic, and the back-end (execution phase) is orderly and more predictable.

This is in line with this insightful definition brought to life by author Steven Pressfield in his blog, *What is 'Female?'* His story idea is that "the female carries the mystery." What could be a better fit for innovation? Innovation is mystery: you don't know where to start, and you have no idea of where you're going.

Here are some beautiful quotes from his readers: for instance, Amber:

Then I understood that it wasn't female as a gender, but female as the concept. The feminine pull vs the masculine push.

Or Andrea Reima:

The feminine is chaos, the masculine is order. But ["the] female carries the mystery" is a more nuanced understanding of chaos. Well, she does conceive, carry, and give birth, but it is a complete mystery how the conception took place, what is developing in utero, and what specific impact that offspring will have, right? [22]

In one of her famous books, late anthropologist Françoise Héritier describes how Aristotle explains the inherent feminine weakness and its "cold" and "humid" nature due to the regular blood losses women regularly incur and of which they have no control over. The masculine has historically been considered superior to the feminine; Héritier interprets that it boils down to "controllable vs uncontrollable."[23]

Lack of control could be considered a weakness in regular life. In innovation, it turns into a strength. Indeed, true innovation is by definition uncontrollable, so being comfortable dealing with situations you cannot really control might be a plus for the feminine in innovation.

This supports my hypotheses that:

- Genuine creative work comes from the feminine.
- We cannot have successful innovation without a collaboration of the masculine and the feminine energies.

This is fighting years of belief that the masculine is the creative force.

---

22   Stephen Pressfield, "What is 'Female?'" *Writing Wednesdays* (blog), *Steven Pressfield*, August 21, 2019.

23   Francoise Héritier, *Masculin/féminin I: La pensée de la différence.* (Paris: OJ.POCHE SC.HU., 2012), chap.1, Kindle.

Héritier outlines biologists' conceptions, which still view life today as the result of "inert" matter (the ovum) being fertilized by an "active" principle (sperm).[24] She cites the *Grand Dictionnaire Universel du XIXe siècle*, 1866–1876:

Women: what is the intellectual inferiority of the woman due to? . . . What does she miss? To produce seeds, meaning ideas [. . .]. No sperm, no seeds, no ideas.[25]

What does neuroscience say?

DOES OUR BRAIN MAKE US MALE OR FEMALE?

There is quite a lot of controversy about the existence of a female brain and a male brain. We still have a lot to discover about the brain, especially when it comes to gender difference, as until recently, about 85 percent of neuroscience research was done exclusively on men.[26]

As bluntly stated by Kelly Cosgrove, associate professor of psychiatry, biomedical imaging, and neuroscience at the Yale School of Medicine:

---

24 Francoise Héritier, *Masculin/féminin I: La pensée de la différence.* (Paris: OJ.POCHE SC.HU., 2012), avant-propos, Kindle.

25 *Encyclopoedia Universalis*, s.v. "Fécondation," 1984, accessed August 26, 2020.

26 Markham Heid, "Biology and the Brain," *Special Time Edition: the Science of Gender,* January 31, 2020, 8.

The field of neuroscience used to approach women as though they were just little men with menstrual cycles.[27]

Indeed, men have been taken as the "by-default" standard for humanity. It may be anecdotal when we talk about designing a bicycle; it can become dramatic when it comes to health and science.

These are key facts:

- Beyond the basic, statistically significant biological differences between men and women, our brains are more similar than different.
- We are not binary beings—we are along a spectrum when it comes to gender, and our brains reflect it: each brain is a unique mosaic of both "male-typical" features and "female-typical" features.
- Our brains have a great plasticity, and neuroplasticity depends on the environment in which we live.
- Key gender differences in the brain are mainly driven by our genome and our hormones.

Gender all starts in the womb. Testosterone is produced at around eight weeks of gestation. Before that, we are all unsexed, with genitals that haven't turned into penises or vaginas.[28]

---

27   Markham Heid, "Biology and the Brain," *Special Time Edition: the Science of Gender,* January 31, 2020, 11.

28   Jeanette Beebe, "Fueling Gender," *Special Time Edition: the Science of Gender,* January 31, 2020, 19.

At the TEDWomen 2018 conference, I had the pleasure of meeting Karissa Sanbonmatsu, a structural biologist at Los Alamos Laboratory. Karissa is a brilliant and humble scientist. She is transgender.

She explains that *"The precursor genitals transform into either female or male during the first trimester of pregnancy. The precursor brains, on the other hand, transform into female or male during the second trimester of pregnancy. So, the current working model is that a unique mix in my mom's womb caused the precursor genitals to transform one way, but the precursor brain to transform the other way."* [29]

The brain is in fact a mosaic made of many female-typical and male-typical patches.

I love this quote from Gina Rippon, professor of cognitive neuroimaging at Aston University, talking about her book *Gender and Our Brains:*

In fact, I wanted to call my book Fifty Shades of Gray Matter.[30]

It graphically and humorously illustrates the continuum of the feminine and the masculine.

---

29   *GRAZ*, "Karissa Sanbonmatsu: What does it mean to be a woman?" January 19, 2020, video, 25:56.

30   Markham Heid, "Biology and the Brain," *Special Time Edition: the Science of Gender,* January 31, 2020, 15.

OUR ENVIRONMENT INFLUENCES
THE MASCULINE/FEMININE BALANCE

Our brains have a great plasticity indeed; they are designed to change in response to the environment. Neuroplasticity depends on socialization. As stated by neuroscientist Gina Rippon:

A gendered world produces a gendered brain.

It all starts in childhood.

Rippon adds: *"Children are like little sponges, and it starts early. Little boys quickly pick up the fact that they shouldn't cry."*[31]

During our interview, Raj Sisodia—who we met in previous chapter—made a very pertinent statement about child energy: *"I think what happens with boys and girls is different. . . . girls, I think, are in their own natural [creative] element until ten or eleven. And then the social pressures and conforming to the patriarchy [happen] and they start to lose themselves along the way."*

"We have research showing that girls are more attuned to other people's emotions, not because of any hardwired difference, but because adults are more likely to say to girls: 'Well, think about how the other person would feel,'" says psychologist Lisa Damour.[32]

---

31   Laura Entis, "From Classroom To Work," *Special Time Edition: the Science of Gender,* January 31, 2020, 54.

32   Ibid.

I was brought up between two brothers. My dad was in the army, and my mom, although very loving, was not particularly maternal. In my education, I was directed toward sciences and mathematics, so I grew up in a male environment. This is why I developed my masculine side to thrive in that context: as a young adult, I was hanging out with the guys, drinking beer, and showing off riding my big motorcycle. I could feel empathy and nurturing stirring deep inside, but it was not appropriate to express them at that time. It was only later in life that I reconnected to my feminine energy, thanks to beautiful encounters, including meeting my husband. And I must say that I am far happier today than I was in my 20s, as I feel more centered and rooted as a human being.

Two specific events shook me and started my journey of reconnection to my feminine side. The first one was a warning on masculinity and the second a call for femininity.

I was working on my PhD in an agro-chemisty laboratory in Toulouse, in the south of France; I was in my 20s. It was a beautiful fall afternoon. A friend burst into the lab: *"Hey, we're going for a coffee at our usual place, they have a big terrace, it will be great with this nice weather, will you join?"* I rode a motorcycle at that time, a Honda XZ 550. I had my leather outfit but didn't put my boots on because it was just a short trip.

I arrived at the café. The terrace was crowded, and I parked just in front, and as usual I got a lot of attention as a skinny girl on a big black motorcycle with gold stripes. I took my time to take off my gloves and helmet—enjoying the ritual and the moment—and joined my friends at their table. We had a good time talking, laughing. At one point it was time to leave. I slowly went through the same ritual, fully conscious that all eyes were on me. My friends had shown me how to accelerate while abruptly releasing the clutch, which made the motorcycle jumpstart. I decided to use that trick to impress the crowd.

Before I knew it, the 220kg motorcycle was up in the air and fell directly on me with the hot exhaust pipe on my leg (remember, I didn't have my boots). Of course, people rushed to help, lifted the motorcycle, and asked me how I was. The burn was only superficial, but my ego was profoundly hurt.

I was wondering what happened when a guy pointed to my front wheel: I had forgotten to take the safety chain off the wheel when I left! As we say in French, "Luckily ridicule doesn't kill. . . ." Needless to say, my next departure was soft and low-profile.

This made me pause and think how stupid I had been to show off like that. Who did I want to impress? What was the point? It was a great lesson in humility.

A few years later, I was hanging out with some male friends at one of our favorite bars in the center of Toulouse. I was not riding my motorcycle, so we were drinking beer and having sort of a "guys talk."

I hadn't noticed that the waiter, a young guy, had a crush on me. At one point, he came towards us and gave me a rose across the counter. I could just see the mocking smiles and smirks on my friends' faces from the corner of my eyes. As I didn't want to show weakness and look ridiculous, I just brushed it away, saying: *"No, thank you."*

The waiter looked at me—I still remember the pain in his eyes—and slowly ate the rose petals in front of me before returning to his work.

I felt something moving deep in my heart: a cry for some compassion, softness, love, gratitude, a call to let it go and be who I really was. The day after, I came back to apologize. The waiter looked at me and said: *"It's your problem to solve,"* and turned his back to me.

A lot of women have similar experiences at hiding their femininity to fit a masculine environment.

Christy Curtis, a yoga and mindfulness guide, told me about her struggle at balancing the feminine and the masculine in her life: *"I was an athletic director for ten years at the high school. I was an administrator; I learned to play hardball to be like one of the guys. Told myself that I can do this, was in people's faces, proving myself, there was a lot of ego . . . and then I realized, no wonder I hate my life because I can't even like myself. There was no alignment with who I was: there lived this softer, feminine, very sensitive empath inside of me who pretended to have a hardened false shell. This is when I crumbled."*

This shows how our masculine or feminine behavior is highly influenced by our environment and the people we meet.

FEMININITY/MASCULINITY IS GENDER AGNOSTIC

Gregory Keyes is a virology systems engineer who worked for years in big corporations. He is now chief eValidation Officer at Conceptual Integrity Group LLC. In our interview, he shared that he grew up in a house with a lot of women including four sisters, so he was brought up in a very feminine environment in contrast to me. In his career, he put his feminine traits to action by helping people succeed—especially women—acting behind the scenes. But he realized that *"The high-powered women I was working with were suddenly moving up, leaving me behind in my career."*

Peju Onile-Ere is a professional in e-commerce and digital innovation. Early in her career, she was working for a company with a total lack of empathy that was extremely demanding of their employees. She noticed: *"It's funny, because it's a digital world, people don't think the people mattered as much: they think it's all digital."* The team manager was a tough woman. One girl, a colleague of Peju, was going through a very rough patch in her personal life. She went to talk to the manager, thinking that as a female manager she would be more understanding. The manager didn't accept what she saw as a "weakness" in another woman, and on the contrary laid a lot more work on the girl. The situation worsened, despite the girl reporting the situation to HR. She eventually fell sick and left the company, along with three other people from the team.

Remember Sis from the previous chapter, the gruff lady with the dangling cigarette who taught Anne Hoag how to knit her Chanel jacket? Like Steve Jobs, she didn't have anything blatantly feminine about her, but she applied her innate feminine traits of empathy, nurturing, and collaboration to create an impactful business. If the feminine traits necessary for innovation are not linked to being a man or a woman, they are neither related to a person's overall look or behavior.

This illustrates that the masculine and the feminine can manifest in any individual, regardless of their position in the gender spectrum, their looks, or their behavior.

To Simon Sinek's point:

What's lacking in the world right now is not women leaders, but rather leaders who lead like women.[33]

SOME DIFFERENCES IN THE MALE/FEMALE BRAIN ARE KEY FOR INNOVATION

The brain differences that allow the masculine and the feminine energies to bring different contributions to innovation can be summarized by:

- Communication between the two brain hemispheres
- Use of grey and white matter
- Processing chemicals, especially hormones.

---

33   Jana Kasperkevic, "Women Leaders: Stop Trying to Lead Like a Man: To be a true leader, you must establish trust and build bonds with your employees, says Simon Sinek," *Inc.*, May 8, 2013.

HEMISPHERIC CONNECTIVITY IS LINKED TO COMMUNICATION

According to a 2014 study, "the brains of males tend to show more 'within-hemispheric' connectivity, while the brains of females display more 'between-hemispheric' connectivity. Overall, results suggest that male brains are structured to facilitate connectivity between perception and coordinated action, whereas female brains are designed to facilitate communication between analytical and intuitive processing modes."[34]

This explains what we covered in Chapter 1: when innovating, men jump from seeing a problem into taking action to solve it, whereas women will analyze the situation and rely on their intuition to connect the dots toward a solution.

Research unveils another aspect of the communication between the two hemispheres: *"Females tend to have verbal centers on both sides of the brain, while males tend to have verbal centers on only the left hemisphere. This is a significant difference. Women tend to use more words when discussing or describing incidence, story, person, object, feeling, or place. Men not only have fewer verbal centers in general but also, often, have less connectivity between their word centers and their memories or feelings. When it comes to discussing feelings and emotions and senses together, women tend to have*

---

34   Madhura Ingalhalikar, Alex Smith, Drew Parker, Theodore D. Satterthwaite, Mark A. Elliott, Kosha Ruparel, Hakon Hakonarson, Raquel E. Gur, Ruben C. Gur, and Ragini Verma, "Sex differences in the structural connectome of the human brain," PNAS January 14, 2014 111 (2) 823-828.

an advantage, and they tend to have more interest in talking about these things."[35]

When I arrived in the US in the early '90s, as part of my immersion into the American culture, I attended a lot of Broadway shows. One of them is still in my head and heart. If I feel blue, I just need to visualize some scenes to have a smile on my face.

The show is *Defending the Caveman* from Rob Becker. It's the longest-running solo show in Broadway history. It explains relationships between men and women in a very funny and loving way.

"The differences that set men and women against each other, [Becker] posits, are based on the primitive past: man's function as hunter, woman's as gatherer. Because a hunter must focus almost maniacally on one thing while a gatherer takes in the details of entire landscapes, men tend to simplify and go directly to the point, while women wool-gather, scramble, synthesize and come to their own, often idiosyncratic conclusions." [36]

I think the following quote perfectly illustrates the difference in verbal communication between men and women:

---

35   Gregory L. Jantz, "Brain Differences Between Genders," *Psychology Today*, February 27, 2014.

36   Juliet Wittman, "Defending the Caveman explains the male of the species," *Westford*, September 26, 2013.

If a guy calls me just to talk, I owe him money.[37]

Expressing feelings and emotions is absolutely key for innovation. Indeed, we will see in Chapter 9 how empathy is critical for innovation. Empathy cannot exist without talking to people and asking questions to understand their feelings. Our feminine side definitely has an advantage here.

GREY MATTER HELPS WITH "FOCUS," WHITE MATTER WITH "CONNECTING THE DOTS"

The male brain utilizes nearly seven times more *grey matter* for activity, while female brains utilize nearly ten times more *white matter*. What does this mean?

"Grey matter areas . . . are information- and action-processing centers . . . white matter is the networking grid that connects the brain's grey matter and other processing centers with one another. The grey-white matter difference may explain why, in adulthood, females are great multi-taskers [although multitasking doesn't exist, the brain is just quickly switching from one task to the other], *while men excel in highly task-focused projects."* [38]

Let's go back to our *Defending the Caveman* show that perfectly explains the "tunnel-vision" and "multitasking" aspects:

---

37   *eNCA,* "Still defending the caveman," March 8, 2019, video, 6:04.

38   Gregory L. Jantz, "Brain Differences Between Genders," *Psychology Today,* February 27, 2014.

A man doesn't just watch the TV. No, a man, he actually becomes the TV. . . . Riya will try and talk to me because, I mean, she knows that she can read a paper and talk to me at the same time. Yeah, must be nice, I have to put my finger down.

Masculine "tunnel vision" versus feminine "connecting dots" is further reinforced here. This outlines the importance of both the feminine and the masculine in innovation.

We're now coming to one of my preferred parts of being a chemist.

PROCESSING CHEMICALS—PARTICULARLY HORMONES—DETERMINE THE FEMININE AND THE MASCULINE

Dramatic changes happen at puberty with the surge of androgens (male hormones) and estrogens (female hormones). Changes happen in the brain, especially in the amygdala, the portion of the brain that processes emotions.[39]

Some dominant neurochemicals are *serotonin*, which, among other things, helps us sit still; *testosterone*, our sex and aggression chemical; *estrogen*, a female growth and reproductive chemical; and *oxytocin*, a bonding-relationship chemical.

In part because of differences in processing these chemicals, males on average tend to be more physically impulsive and aggressive. Additionally, men process less of the bonding

------

39   Jeanette Beebe, "Fueling Gender," *Special Time Edition: The Science of Gender*, January 31, 2020, 19.

chemical oxytocin, known as the "cuddle chemical," than women.[40]

Another chemical that's key, according to two studies from University of Pennsylvania, is Foxp2 protein, which is more present in women than men. That explains why women speak twenty thousand words per day versus seven thousand for men and why women would be better at communication.[41]

Those facts explain what we saw in Chapter 1: men jump to conclusions, and women take the time to stay still and process the information. This is absolutely key for intuition, as we will discover in Chapter 11. Women are also better at communicating, which is a prerequisite to successful innovation.

BRAIN PLASTICITY ALLOWS US TO DEVELOP AND ACTIVATE OUR FEMININITY OR OUR MASCULINITY

Brain plasticity depends on environment, as described by Gina Rippon: they witnessed an increase of oxytocin blood levels and the falling of testosterone in new fathers (or adopting parents) when they are in the physical presence of their babies. The father of a newborn baby who is the primary caregiver of the baby will have a much lower testosterone level than the father who is not the primary caregiver.[42]

---

40   Gregory L. Jantz, "Brain Differences Between Genders," *Psychology Today*, February 27, 2014.

41   Fiona Macrae, "Women talk more than men due to higher levels of Foxp 2 protein," *news.com.au*, February 21, 2013.

42   Markham Heid, "Biology and the Brain," *Special Time Edition: The Science of Gender*, January 31, 2020, 15.

IT ALL BOILS DOWN TO EMOTIONS

Research found that women are better at recognizing facial effects, expression processing, and emotions in general, with an overall female advantage in nonverbal emotional recognition across 215 samples.[43]

The female brain, in part thanks to far more natural blood flow throughout the brain at any given moment (more white matter processing), will often ruminate on and revisit emotional memories more than the male brain.

Males tend, after reflecting more briefly on an emotive memory, to analyze it somewhat and then move onto the next task.

Thus, observers may mistakenly believe that boys avoid feelings in comparison to girls or move to problem solving too quickly.[44]

'***'

We now understand that:

- Our brains are a mosaic of female and male patches that's unique to each individual, placing us on our distinctive spot on the gender continuum.

---

43   M.E. Kret and B. de Gelder, "A review on sex differences in processing emotional signals," *Neuropsychologia* 50, no.7 (2012): 1211-1221.

44   Bruce Goldman, "Two minds: The cognitive differences between men and women," *Stanford Medicine*: Sex, gender and Medicine, Spring 2017.

- If male and female brains are mostly similar, some key physiological differences are emphasized by education and the environment.
- Our brains' plasticity allows any individual along the gender spectrum to round up their innovation profile by acquiring the complementary skills.

That way, the feminine and the masculine energies work together to bring their unique contribution to successful innovation.

3

INNOVATION HAS NEGLECTED WOMEN

———

In the 17th century, "innovators" didn't get accolades. They got their ears cut off.

EMMA GREEN, STAFF WRITER AT THE ATLANTIC.

It doesn't really entice anyone to venture into innovation, does it? This may be part of the answer to the critical question:

WHY AREN'T THERE MORE WOMEN IN INNOVATION?

I identified several factors. To confirm, let's have a look at the history of women's roles in society and in the workforce.

INNOVATION IS FOR REBELS AND ADVENTURERS

Green goes back to the history of innovation. In the 17th century, "'innovation' wasn't a compliment. It was an accusation.

In fact, shouts of 'Innovator!' used to be akin to charges of heresy."[45]

"From the 1400s through the 1600s, prior to early American settlement, the concept of 'innovation' was pejorative. It was an early modern synonym for rebellion, revolt and heresy."[46]

What's quite fascinating is that there is something left from this trauma in our modern era, even if it took a more positive turn. How many times do we hear that innovators are rebels or outliers?

Hell, there are no rules here—we're trying to accomplish something.

THOMAS EDISON.

"This quote from the foremost inventor of his generation resonates with the essence of Innovation. From a cultural perspective, however, with respect to organizations, this conflict [breaking the rules] *represents a huge challenge."* [47]

It wasn't certainly my case, but because of their brain biology and more importantly their upbringing and education, girls have a tendency to be quieter, stay still, and conform. Boys are encouraged to be adventurous go-getters.

---

45   Emma Green, "Innovation: The History of a Buzzword," *The Atlantic,* June 13, 2013.

46   "Innovation vs Renovation," *Ask Difference,* Published August 13, 2020.

47   Paul Meyers, "Managing and Communicating Innovation in a Startup," *Medium,* April 3, 2020.

Boys are taught to be brave, while girls are taught to be perfect.

RESHMA SAUJANI, FOUNDER OF GIRLS WHO CODE
AND AUTHOR OF BRAVE, NOT PERFECT.

Historically and culturally, innovation seemed to be more suited to men's temperaments than women's.

INNOVATION WAS BORN IN SCIENCE AND TECHNOLOGY
Innovation was rooted in science and industry during the nineteenth century Industrial Revolution. Innovation was defined as technical invention. It was only in 1939 that the Austrian economist Joseph Schumpeter gave innovation its business dimension.

This very rational approach grounded in technology left women out of the innovation field, as science and technology have historically been domains from which women were mostly excluded.

It started well in several early civilizations with the involvement of women in the field of medicine. The study of natural philosophy in ancient Greece was open to women. They contributed to the proto-science of alchemy in the first or second centuries AD. During the Middle Ages, convents were an important place of education for women, even if they faced serious biases: for example, St. Thomas Aquinas, a Christian scholar, wrote, referring to women: *"She is mentally incapable of holding a position of authority."*

Then, with the emergence of the first universities in the eleventh century, women were, for the most part, excluded from university education.[48]

Throughout the centuries, although women excelled in many scientific areas, they have been kept away from science for all the wrong reasons. The case of Carl Linnaeus' system of plant classification based on sexual characteristics is a good example. People *"feared that women would learn immoral lessons from nature's example... Women were often depicted as both innately emotional and incapable of objective reasoning."*[49]

By the eighteenth century, Laura Bassi was the first woman to earn a professorship in physics at the University of Bologna, earning recognition for women in science. Marie Curie was the only woman to win two Nobel prizes, in 1903 (physics) and 1911 (chemistry).

I had to impose myself as a female scientist and was hoping it would get far easier for the young generation. However, according to a 2020 publication of the World Economic Forum:

- Female students and employees are under-represented in fields related to STEM (science, technology, engineering, and math).

---

48 Leigh Ann Whaley, *Women's History as Scientists* (Santa Barbara, California: ABC-CLIO, INC.), 2003.

49 Ruth Watts, *Women in Science: A Social and Cultural History*, London and New York: Rootledge, 2007, 63.

- On average, around 30 percent of the world's researchers are women.
- Less than a third of female students choose to study higher education courses in subjects like math and engineering.[50]

As a result, in 2017, just 9.2 percent of the US patents that were granted were made by female inventors.[51]

As I unfortunately witnessed, the lack of women in scientific research translates into the professional world. In 2020:

- Only 20 percent of all tech jobs are held by women.
- Twenty-six percent of all computing jobs in the world are held by women.
- Five percent of startup founders are women.
- The quit rate for women in STEM is 53 percent.[52]

**WOMEN SUFFER FROM A LACK OF
VISIBILITY AND SUPPORT IN STEM**

An overlooked strategy to stop the departure of senior women in STEM is to make sure they have the right kind of visibility within the organization. Visibility is about valued technical

---

50   Johnny Wood, "3 things to know about women in STEM11 Feb 2020," *World Economic Forum,* February 11, 2020.

51   Bob Stembridge, "Women in Innovation: Gaining Ground, but Still Far Behind," *Scientific American,* May 3, 2018.

52   Darina Lynkova, "Women in Technology Statistics: What's new in 2020?" *techjury,* June 22, 2020.

and leadership skills, as well as visibility in assignments and networks.[53]

There is a similar lack of recognition in academics. *"Junior female scientists aren't getting the credit they deserve"*. As a result, *"women earn about half of the doctoral degrees in science, yet they represent a mere 21 percent of the faculty at the full professor level at research institutions in the United States."* [54]

WOMEN SUFFER FROM GENDER BIAS IN HIRING

I was fortunate to have corporate mentors and champions who recognized my unique value and helped me pave the way to my career. It is not the case of all women, though, and there were instances where I had to fight to remain true to who I was, as corporations have a tendency to teach women to *fit the existing mold.*

I was in an intercompany innovation meeting. Waiting for the session to start, I was joking and laughing with my newly met neighbor. I need to specify that I wore one of my boldly colored outfits. The facilitator (an older white man) was going through the attendees list. As we were about to start, he said: *"I don't see Dr. Jacquet; we may want to wait as we*

---

53   Shelley J. Correll and Lori Mackenzie, "To Succeed in Tech, Women Need More Visibility," *Harvard Business Review,* September 13, 2016.

54   Marc J. Lerchenmueller and Olav Sorenson, "Research: Junior Female Scientists Aren't Getting the Credit They Deserve," *Harvard Business Review,* March 22, 2017.

need technology representation." I looked at him right in the eyes: *"I am Dr. Jacquet."*

The look on his face was priceless. For sure, I didn't fit the mold of a "serious scientist," and I am quite sure he wouldn't have hired me.

Fitting the mold inherently discourages innovation.

There had been some progress in the hiring of women in the technology field in the last few years, however, in 2020 there was a setback with the COVID-19 pandemic.

The percentage of women hired has dropped since the pandemic, especially in entertainment, finance, and technology, erasing the gains of the previous two years:

"The engine of hiring bias is decision makers [who feel] more confident hiring people who remind them of themselves. At a moment when there are a lot of external stressors, that search for comfort by the decision maker—sometimes conscious and sometimes not—could kick into a slightly higher drive."[55]

THERE ARE NOT ENOUGH WOMEN CEOS AND OTHER DECISION ROLES IN BIG COMPANIES

Innovation will not happen in a company unless it is championed by the C-suite.

---

55   Caroline Fairchild, "These male-dominated industries were hiring more women. Then COVID-19 happened," *LinkedIn News,* June 17, 2020.

Unfortunately, the C-suite has been predominantly masculine:

- Globally, 29 percent of senior management roles are held by women; however, 43 percent of human resources directors are women compared to 17 percent of sales directors and 16 percent of chief information officers. It is clearly not in HR that the key decisions are made for the future of business and innovation.
- The situation varies geographically: in 2017 in India, women held only 7 percent of senior management (CEO/managing director) roles. In Canada, women continue to hold 10 percent of C-Level executive roles. In Europe, among the largest publicly listed companies in the European Union (EU-28) in 2019, only 17.6 percent of executives and 6.9 percent of CEOs were women.
- It is very revealing to see that in the US, in S&P 500 companies, the higher up the corporate ladder, the fewer the women: 44.7 percent of total employees are women, with 26.5 percent at the executive/senior level, and only 5 percent as CEOs.[56]

How can women help shape the future of the world when they are not in the position to make the decisions that will impact the future of our world?

Another phenomenon I observed is that senior businesspeople get top innovation jobs as a reward for their business accomplishments when it's not a sort of preretirement job. It also happens that those people are mainly men. It doesn't

---

56   "Women in Management: Quick Take," Catalyst, accessed August 11, 2020.

make sense, as we saw that innovation requires specific skills or at least a mindset that is not really aligned with the attributes needed in business.

This situation can be seen up to the board level.

Corporate boards suffer from a lack of expertise in innovation: *"Many directors—particularly CEOs—express frustration that their boards lack the level of industry expertise and innovation experience necessary to make well-informed risk-reward assessments about proposals."* [57] Globally, men occupy more board seats than women. As of 2018, women held 20.8 percent of the board seats on Russell 1000 companies.[58]

So, structurally, women are often left out of the corporate innovation world.

INNOVATION IS STILL DOMINATED BY MASCULINE ENERGY

According to WIN (Women in Innovation), which started in 2016 in response to a gender gap in the innovation field:

- Only 25 percent of the top innovation firms are led by women.

---

57 Linda A. Hill and George Davis, "The Board's New Innovation Imperative," *Harvard Business Review,* from the November–December 2017 Issue.

58 2020 Women on Board, "Accelerating Women into Corporate Boardrooms," Home page, Accessed August 22, 2020.

- In 2018, women accounted for only 20 percent of Fortune 500 Chief Innovation Officers.[59]

My friend and business partner Kaylie Dugan, a longtime consultant to Fortune 500 companies, made a great observation about the corporate masculine aspect being counterproductive to innovation: *"In order to really excel in large companies, we must be logical. No, we must never laugh; no, we must never have fun."*

Kaylie and I, however, conducted several successful projects together in different product categories and cultures—each time we worked hard and got results; we also had a lot of fun.

The current corporate definition of success implies some "masculine" behaviors that don't foster an innovative climate:

- *"Show no weakness": a workplace that demands swaggering confidence, never admitting doubt or mistakes, and suppressing any tender or vulnerable emotions ("no sissy stuff").*
- *"Put work first": a workplace where nothing outside the organization (e.g., family) can interfere with work, where taking a break or a leave represents an impermissible lack of commitment.*

---

59   Women In Innovation, "WIN's Founding Story," Founding story page, Accessed August 22, 2020.

- *"Dog eat dog": a workplace filled with ruthless competition, where "winners" (the most masculine) focus on defeating "losers" (the less masculine), and no one is trusted.*[60]

My experience is that the essence of meaningful innovation is doubting, asking questions, making mistakes, and listening to emotions. There is a need for personal time to recharge our brain and energy. In addition, as innovative ideas can come from any place, we need to stay open and connected to the world outside of our own work universe. The best innovation is based on collaboration, which requires trust and support for others.

Women have been kept outside of the innovation world. Is it justified, or can the feminine bring value to innovation?

WOMEN ARE UNSUNG INVENTORS AND CREATORS

Katherine Johnson is the brilliant mind behind the success of NASA's first US manned space flight, as her calculations played a crucial role in it. She was finally rewarded the Presidential Medal of Freedom in 2015 at ninety-six years old. Her achievements became more popular thanks to the 2016 movie *Hidden Figures*.

---

60   Jennifer L. Berdahl, Peter Glick and Marianne Cooper, "How Masculinity Contests Undermine Organizations, and What to Do About It," *Harvard Business Review*, November 02, 2018.

The movie highlights how hard she had to fight with her colleagues to be listened to as women of color, despite their brilliancy and significant contributions.[61]

A recurrent theme is how women's inventions were attributed to men—not that they did it intentionally, it was just the way society was.

Widely regarded as the world's first computer programmer, Augusta Ada King-Noel, Countess of Lovelace, was a nineteenth-century mathematician and writer. She paved the way for Alan Turing's work on the first modern computers during World War II.

She worked with a partner, inventor Charles Babbage, and the two came up with an idea for an "Analytical Machine." In 1843, she wrote notes that basically were the invention of computer programming. But for years, historians assumed Babbage had written them.

Born in 1915, Hedwig Eva Maria Kiesler was an Austrian actress better known as Hollywood star Hedy Lamarr. She was the epitome of beauty—and she was also a prolific inventor. During World War II, she invented and patented a frequency-hopping signal that was impossible to hack to avoid radio-controlled torpedoes to be knocked off course. She invented wireless communication, but the US government refused to take her seriously.

---

61   Olivia Tambini, "10 female tech innovators you may not have heard of," *Techradar,* August 2018.

The US Navy classified her original patent and filed it away—until they gradually began developing technologies based on it, giving zero credit to her.[62]

It is also true in another domain at the intersection of creativity and invention: art.

Suzanne Valadon was known for modeling for Pierre-Auguste Renoir and Henri de Toulouse-Lautrec, though she was an artist herself. Camille Claudel was an exceptionally talented artist, but as a woman, she couldn't make a name of her own. She had to collaborate with Auguste Rodin and let him get the credit as the "lionized figure of French sculptures." Rodin obviously signed a number of her works.[63]

This is how Laure Adler, journalist, author and historian, introduces her book. *The Trouble with Women Artists— Reframing the History of Art.* I love it because you can replace the word "art" with "innovation":

"One is not born an artist, but rather becomes one. Since its beginnings, the history of art has been conceived, written, published, and taught by men. And when you are born as a woman, being an artist is a perilous, never-ending fight, and physically, intellectually and mentally exhausting. Today, the time has come to reframe and reexamine the creative works

62 Melina Glusac, "14 world-changing innovations by women that were originally credited to men," *Insider,* Mar 8, 2020.

63 Google Arts & Culture, "The Women Painters Overlooked By Art History," Editorial Feature, Accessed August 22, 2020.

of those women who have had the courage to defy the rules in order to fulfill their calling.[64]

'***'

In this chapter, we established that innovation is still dominated by the masculine energy and that it's difficult for women to find their place: for centuries, women had limited access to science and technology. As these were the foundation for innovation, women also had limited access to innovation. Another factor is the lack of women in decision roles and high-level innovation positions in corporations. There are also sociocultural reasons that held women behind, as illustrated by the artistic world.

We will now try to understand how innovation could be improved.

---

64   Laure Adler and Camille Viéville, *"The Trouble with Women Artists: Reframing the History of Art,"* Paris: Flammarion, 2019, book cover.

4

WHAT INNOVATION NEEDS MORE OF TODAY

———

A record of our emotional life
is written on our hearts.

This is an excerpt from cardiologist Sandeep Jauhar's stunning TED talk. He explores the mysterious ways our emotions impact the health of our hearts.

EMOTIONS ARE POWERFUL

Jauhar demonstrates how emotions are so powerful that they can alter the physiological shape of our heart. Its shape changes in response to grief or fear, and it can literally break in response to emotional heartbreak.[65]

———

65   *TED Talks,* "Sandeep Jauhar: How your emotions change the shape of your heart," July 2019, video, 15:54.

I experienced firsthand the impact of emotions in my personal life.

On a beautiful day in summer 2009, a friend of ours came to our home to buy a painting from my husband Patrick, a self-made artist and painter.

In 2007, Patrick was diagnosed with lung cancer and went through two very tough years between the surgery and the chemo treatment. Then one day, he had enough physical and mental strength to grab the brush and paint again. Usually it takes Patrick weeks to complete a painting, but he did this one in a record time, with a sort of frenzy. He called it *Hymn to Life*.

Our friend had already bought some paintings from Patrick. That day, we lined up around ten paintings in our living room. Usually he hesitated between several options, but that day, I hadn't even finished lining up the canvases when he just blurted out: *"This is the one I want,"* pointing to Patrick's latest work (he didn't know it was the latest one, and we didn't share the title). This gave me chills, and I asked: *"Why this one, and why are you so sure?"* He answered: *"Because it resonates with me, when I look at it I feel both despair and hope. . . ."* Wow! Certainly a computer could have artistically and aesthetically done a similar work, but it could never have transferred onto the canvas the emotions Patrick felt when painting.

It illustrates the fact that, if we want innovation that sells, we need to tap into the human and emotional aspects.

CREATIVITY IS WHAT MAKES US HUMAN

People all over the world are getting scared of technology and wondering if and when robots will take over their jobs. Fortunately, we are reminded that:

Creativity is, in fact, the unique and defining trait of our [human] species.
PULITZER PRIZE-WINNING BIOLOGIST EDWARD O. WILSON[66]

Creativity is as much part of our tool kit as walking on two legs and having a big brain.
ANTHROPOLOGIST AUGUSTIN FUENTES[67]

So, emotions are at the origin of creativity, and creativity is the precursor of innovation and of what makes us human. It starts to all come together, doesn't it?

It points to the fact that our humanity and emotions are the engine of innovation.

MOST ORGANIZATIONS OVERLOOK THE POWER OF EMOTIONS, AND THUS HUMANITY

In companies, innovation is unfortunately often handled as a business. Human creativity and emotions are left out to favor processes and productivity. Emotions are not taken

---

66   Richard Jerome, "Striving For The New," *Special Time Edition: the Science of Creativity,* August 3, 2018, 6.

67   Ibid.

seriously in business, despite the fact that they make the difference when it comes to consumers' buying decisions, particularly for women.

In his book *Humans Are Underrated*, journalist Geoff Colvin argues that *"As technology advances with increasing speed, the most valuable skills in the economy will be skills of deep human interaction—empathy, creative problem-solving in groups, storytelling—and that developing these skills will be crucial to the futures of individuals, companies, and nations."*

The book shows that while demand for such skills is rising, supply may be falling as our increasingly digital lives cause these skills to atrophy. The imbalance of supply and demand is thus making these skills even more valuable.[68]

In my career, I worked for many years with my friend Marc Somnolet, a seasoned CPG Marketing executive and now an adjunct professor at New York University. This is what he shared about corporate innovation: *"Innovating for the business is the biggest error for many CPG companies. [Innovation] really starts with innovating for people. It's as simple as saying: here are the types of people we would like to find solutions for, go out there and find out what they're all about, as opposed to saying: here are the categories you need to think about and create products for them. In fact, it is about opening your eyes and ears, being empathetic and speaking to somebody without an agenda."*

---

68   "Humans Are Underrated: What High Achievers Know That Brilliant Machines Never Will By Geoff Colvin," Penguin Random House, accessed August 29, 2020.

In our interview, Marc made the point that when companies innovate for the business, *"at best, they come up with very small, incremental ideas to their current business . . . oftentimes they aren't even incremental; they're purely cannibalistic. With this new method of looking at empathy and other [feminine] traits, now all of a sudden you have a way to develop something that potentially could be awesome, and awesome is a hell of a lot better than just a good innovation."*

When I mentioned emotions, an experience immediately popped into Marc's mind. As a coach in design thinking, he once ran a session with a corporate global legal organization, whose employees could be stereotypically considered as "the least innovative people in the world." He relates how: *"Amazing things happen when you give permission to people to go out there and be creative with no judgments. Then you discover new facets of people."*

The objective of the session was to create an archival system for the legal organization that people would actually use. Doesn't sound exciting, does it? Instead of jumping to technical solutions as had been done in the past, Marc asked them to interview a bunch of people around the world—not limited to the legal profession—to get a different perspective. And what they found was really interesting: the reason why people were not using the archival system was not the data or the system itself—it was the lack of human interaction.

They started to design a system that was more intuitive, with two new features. The first feature allowed the user to connect and exchange with any person in the legal organization at any level. The second and even more important feature was a new onboarding system for the legal professionals hired from outside. This allowed them to get familiar with the corporate system and for the insiders to benefit from new knowledge.

It was a huge success, proving that when you start tapping into human emotions, technology becomes the driver serving a higher purpose instead of being the whole focus of the project.

Lionel Yang, a transformation researcher, is very involved in ESG, which takes into consideration the environmental, social and governance factors alongside financial factors in the investment decision-making process. During our interview, he made very good points on how businesses are run today. The following can be applied to innovation:

"Current economy basically is an economy of competition versus care about other people. The business transformations used to be just process-based, but it should be about transformation in psychology. Ninety percent of [business transformations] fail because the way they are being done is process oriented rather than people.

It's because you have to manage organization with data. You need to measure what you need to improve; for leaders to make a decision, they need data. [Change driven by people] is about awareness. This is something that requires a different kind of leadership skill set. The traditional way of training leaders is like training engineers. . . . No, it's more like being a priest or a psychotherapist."

During my career, I often experienced this tension between business leaders asking for key performance indicators (KPIs) and other success measures and the innovation leaders struggling to deliver. It is especially true for the front-end of innovation.

The return on investment (ROI) in innovation cannot be measured immediately. In business, when you run a promotion, you can evaluate at the end how much you invested in it and the additional revenues you got, hence measuring your ROI.

In innovation, you may invest in a technology, or research, or even a brainstorming session that may pay off years later, which means innovation efficiency has to be evaluated on a longer term.

EMOTIONAL CONNECTION IS WHAT SELLS
Letting people express their emotions creates an environment where creativity can flourish.

This is not the only positive impact of emotions on innovation: creating from your heart and emotions will produce solutions that emotionally connect with your target consumer. As I described in the introduction, I had the living proof in my professional life when we developed a winning shower gel product with a process based on emotions.

Simon Sinek described this beautifully when talking about Apple products: *"We buy [them] because of the 'why,' not the 'what' or 'how,' because of our brain system. When we communicate from the outside in, yes, people can understand vast amounts of complicated information like features, benefits, facts, and figures, but it just doesn't drive behavior. When we can communicate from the inside out, we're talking directly to the part of the brain that controls behavior, and then we allow people to rationalize it with the tangible things we say and do."*[69]

This is where gut decisions come from. It justifies that great innovation comes from emotions.

My friend Lisa Lipkin, the story strategist we met in Chapter 1, confirmed the power of emotions in communication: *"When men, or women for that matter, who aren't particularly connected to their emotions are given access to them, when they're allowed to do that in a workplace setting, not only does it make their delivery better in the corporate presentations, but it opens them up to the people around them. I've seen incredible things; I've really seen magical things happen once people are accessing what moves them emotionally and that really it's transformative in the workplace."*

Lisa shared a specific example: *"I remember working with a financial advisor who had started a family and was changing his business to family financial planning. He was having trouble selling his services. I asked: 'Well, what do you tell your clients?' He answered: 'I'm a family man, I got rid of my Corvette sports car and I bought a minivan.' He kept promoting his idea of being a family man, but it didn't sound authentic to me.*

---

69   *TED Talks,* "Simon Sinek: How great leaders inspire action," September 2009, video, 17:49.

I looked at his watch. I asked him to tell me a story about the watch. This is a trick to get people to connect to a memory, which ultimately helps them connect emotionally to something.

He answered: 'This was my grandfather's.' After a pause: 'I love my grandfather. Every Sunday, I get my Corvette sports car out of the garage and we go to church together.'

I said: 'I thought you got rid of your Corvette.' 'Well, I put it in the garage, but I use it on weekends.' And as he started to talk, I told him: 'Look, rather than being an insufferable 1950s TV dad, you suddenly are much more appealing to me. You're now a guy that goes to church and loves his family but still loves his material objects. Now you become multidimensional; that's to me a winning financial advisor.'

And literally, this guy transformed: it was as if somebody had given him permission to be himself for the first time, and it really helped us turn around his business down the road."

Science backs up the fact that emotions are critical in people's decision-making. Rationality only represents about 20 percent of human decision-making: *"It is said that emotions drive 80% of the choices Americans make, while practicality and objectivity only represent about 20% of decision-making. Without a doubt, our emotions dictate our thoughts, intentions and actions with superior authority to our rational minds."* [70]

---

70 Thomas Oppong, "Psychologists Explain How Emotions, Not logic, Drive Human Behaviour," *Medium*, January 3, 2020.

How to deal with global consumers, as emotions vary depending on the culture?

A new study shows that many aspects of emotions, as well as what triggers certain emotions, vary across different cultures. However, what emotions *feel* like does not seem to be subject to similar kinds of cultural influences.[71] This is absolutely crucial for companies with a global footprint.

Emotions are key for innovating globally by effectively connecting with our consumers, particularly women.

EMOTIONS ARE ESPECIALLY CRITICAL TO INNOVATE FOR THE FEMALE MARKET

In her book *EVEOLUTION*, Faith Popcorn, futurist and CEO at Faith Popcorn's BrainReserve, advocates that:

Women Don't Buy Brands; They Join Them. . . . They want a brand to speak to their heads and hearts. To understand them. To recognize their needs, values, standards and dreams.[72]

---

71   Berit Brogaard, "Do Emotions Feel the Same Across Different Cultures?" *Psychology Today,* January 15, 2020.

72   Faith Popcorn and Lys Marigold, *EVEOLUTION: Understanding women—8 essential truths that work in your business and your life.* (New York: Hyperion, 2000), 4-6.

'✳✳✳'

It is not a surprise that only 6 percent of global executives are satisfied with their innovation performance, according to a McKinsey global survey, although 84 percent agree innovation is critical for business, and 80 percent think current business models are at risk.[73]

For successful innovation to happen in corporations, emotions are needed on top of the processes.

Not only do emotions create a safe and nurturing environment where innovators can express their human creativity, they also deliver innovation that sells by emotionally connecting to consumers.

Emotions are not a handicap in business: they are a power to innovate, especially when it comes to the female consumer. Innovating—particularly for women—doesn't stop at technology and design. It means understanding and accepting people's profound psychological and emotional needs.

---

73   Greg Satell, "4 Ways Leaders Can Get More from Their Company's Innovation Efforts," *HBR*, October 10, 2017.

2

THE OPPORTUNITY
FOR THE FUTURE
OF INNOVATION

5

THE $20+ TRILLION FEMALE MARKET IS AN UNTAPPED OPPORTUNITY

———

A public health challenge doubled the number of American women going to the emergency room between 2002 and 2012, according to a BMC Public Health report in 2017. It causes musculoskeletal pain, venous complaints such as fatigue and heavy-feeling legs, and has been found to provoke venous hypertension in the lower limbs, not to mention long-term aches and pains. In the US this practice affects 70 percent of women at some point in their lives and over 40 percent on a daily basis. Fifty percent of women experience daily pain from it.[74]

And yet women continue to do it.

———

74   Max Barnish, Heather May Morgan and Jean Barnish, "The 2016 High Heels: Health effects And psychosexual Benefits," *BMC Public Health* 18, 37 (2018).

What is this practice that sounds like torture?

Wearing high heels.

WHY ARE HIGH HEELS LABELED FEMININE?

In the medieval period, both men and women wore platform shoes. It was for a very practical reason, though, as a way to elevate them from the trash and excrement-filled streets. Modern high heels appeared in the early seventeenth century. Only men wore them, as a sign of upper-class status. A seventeenth-century law in Massachusetts announced that *"women would be subjected to the same treatment as witches if they lured men into marriage via the use of high-heeled shoes"*!

Then, in the late 1780s, high heels became exclusively feminine and, very interestingly, associated with a woman's supposed sense of impracticality and extravagance. During World War II, the popularization of pin-up girl posters increased the relationship between high heels and female sexuality.

The tall, skinny stiletto heel was invented in the early 1900s by French designers Roger Vivier and André Perugia (sometimes I am a little bit embarrassed to be French). It strengthened the relationship between women, sexuality, and appearance. Block heels then became popular from the 1960s to the 1990s.[75]

---

75 Paul Morris, Jenny White, Edward Morrison and Kayleigh Fisher, "High Heels are Supernormal Stimuli: How Wearing High Heels Affects Judgments of Female Attractiveness," *Evolution and Human Behavior,* 34, 3: 176–181 (May 2013).

When the stiletto made a comeback in the 2000s, women's appearances in emergency rooms dramatically increased.[76]

SO, WHY DO WOMEN STILL WEAR HIGH HEELS?

Paul Morris, a psychology researcher at the University of Portsmouth, argues that *"high heels accentuate 'sex specific aspects of female gait,' artificially increasing a woman's femininity. . . . Emphasis is placed on the appearance of the wearer instead of their arguably more valuable internal traits such as intelligence, creativity, or strength."*[77]

This makes high heels a dilemma to women, as they bring them psychosexual benefits but are detrimental to their health.

Rosabeth Moss Kanter confessed in a *Harvard Business Review* article that: *"[The ancient Chinese practice of foot-binding was imposed on women]. The modern fashion practice of wearing toe-squeezing high-heeled shoes has a voluntary component. Far be it for me to blame the victim, because I, too, fall in line at the fashion parade."*[78]

76   Max Barnish, Heather May Morgan and Jean Barnish, "The 2016 High Heels: Health effects And psychosexual Benefits," *BMC Public Health* 18, 37 (2018).

77   Paul Morris, Jenny White, Edward Morrison and Kayleigh Fisher, "High Heels are Supernormal Stimuli: How Wearing High Heels Affects Judgments of Female Attractiveness," *Evolution and Human Behavior,* 34, 3: 176–181 (May 2013).

78   Rosabeth Moss Kanter, "For International Women's Day, Think Outside the (Shoe)Box," *HBR,* March 7, 2011.

I am guilty too. I had a recent foot surgery. The first thing the surgeon asked me: "Have you been wearing high heels?" The short answer is yes—for my entire adult life, and I wouldn't have even thought otherwise. Like makeup and dyeing your hair, this was part of a woman's regimen, and I never questioned it—until today.

HIGH HEELS HAVE BEEN DESIGNED BY MEN

It is revealing to observe that when men wore heels in the past, is was for very practical reasons. Indeed, the shoes were designed to improve safety during horse-back riding by ensuring the rider's feet stayed in the stirrups. But when it comes to designing high heels for women, suddenly the drivers are fashion and appearance, not comfort and technology.

The women's footwear market is still dominated by men.[79]

I design the [women's] shoes for men, since they are the ones who will appreciate how attractive women will look in them.

This is how Christian Louboutin, a famous shoe designer, describes his inspiration.[80]

79 William Kremer, "Why did men stop wearing high heels?" *BBC News*, January 25, 2013.

80 Elizabeth Segran, "High Heels, Invented For The Male Gaze, Get A Feminist Makeover," *Fast Company*, April 13, 2018.

Men usually design for women from their own perspective. This is one of the key reasons why the female market in general is underserved and represents a huge business opportunity.

It is important to first realize how sizeable this market is to better appreciate the importance of addressing it with the right approach.

THE FEMALE ECONOMY IS A $20+ TRILLION MARKET

A 2017 survey by Merrill Lynch in partnership with Age Wave outlines the not-so-distant past and the progress made by women regarding wealth: "American women couldn't own property (up until 1862), vote (1920) or apply for individual credit cards (1974). Women still make less money (pay gap is above 20 percent). They live longer than men yet accumulate less wealth to fund their longer lives."

However, there has been a dramatic increase in women's earnings, which grew by 75 percent compared to only 5 percent for men between 1970 and 2015.[81]

As a result, women now drive the world economy.

According to *Frost & Sullivan,* the female economy is poised to outpace the economy of some of the biggest nations in the next five years, representing a growth market bigger than China and India combined. The global female income

---

81   Merrill Lynch, "Women & Financial Wellness: Beyond the Bottom Line," Study in partnership with Age Wave, October 25–November 22, 2017.

reached $24 trillion annually in 2020, up from $20 trillion in 2018.

Women control $43 trillion of global consumer spending. Women-owned companies represent over 40 percent of registered businesses worldwide in 2020.[82] Fifty-one percent of personal wealth in the US is controlled by women.[83]

Harvard Business Review describes how the greatest market potential lies in six industries. Four are businesses where "women are most likely to spend more or trade up:" fitness, food, apparel, and beauty. The other two are businesses with which women "have made their dissatisfaction very clear": financial services and health care.[84]

Women over fifty—the "elastic generation"—have a significant buying power that is still ignored today, and women of color also represent a growth opportunity.

FITNESS

The US health club industry revenue increased to $32.3 billion in 2018, up from $30 billion in 2017, a 7.8 percent growth.[85]

82 New Jersey Business, "Global Female Income to Reach $24 Trillion in 2020," *NJB Magazine,* March 6, 2020.

83 Yie-Hsin Hung, "51% of personal wealth in the U.S. is controlled by women," *WealthTrack,* June 28, 2019.

84 Michael J. Silverstein and Kate Sayre, "The Female Economy," *HBR,* from the September 2009 Issue.

85 IHRSA Staff, "2018 Shows Continuing Uptrend of U.S. Health Club Industry," *IHRSA,* April 12, 2019.

There are opportunities for innovating ways to create no-frills fitness chains as witnessed by the success of Curves. For over twenty-five years, it has been a proven business model designed especially for women, offering a supportive, welcoming, and safe environment.[86]

There is also a need for exercise that focuses less on performance and looks and more on feeling good and exercising at your level without pressure.

I have been seduced by *Yoga with Adriene* and her (assistant) dog Benji, thanks to her no-fuss, authentic, and caring attitude. Well, it also generates business: "Her YouTube channel has over 10 million subscribers as of 2020 and has accumulated over 900 million views so far. It should generate an estimated revenue of $7,000 per day ($2.5 million a year) from the ads that appear on the videos."[87]

BEAUTY

The 2020 COVID-19 pandemic accelerated an existing trend toward skincare versus beauty care. Women want to boost their immune system. They focus on a natural look and authenticity. Beauty often involves an egocentric and relentless seeking of perfection. In the future, women want to privilege how they "feel" vs how they "look."

---

86   Curves, accessed August 30, 2020.

87   Julian, "How Much Money Yoga With Adriene Makes On YouTube – Net Worth," *Naibuzz,* last Updated on: April 14, 2020.

I had the pleasure of interviewing Anna Moine, a spa industry insider and retail innovator. I like how she sees the future values in the beauty industry: *"simplicity, sustainability, clarity, inclusivity, and sincerity."*[88]

Actually, fitness, beauty, and health are converging into wellness, now a $4.2 trillion global industry.[89]

FEMALE WELLNESS

The Global Wellness Institute has identified the trend: *"A New [Female] Wellness—from women-only clubs and co-working spaces—to a FemTech wave that solves for women's bodies and lives—to more wellness travel aimed at women's empowerment—to women of color moving the industry beyond #WellnessSoWhite. [Female] wellness is dominated by female founders, with a woman-to-woman brand approach that's more chatty, inclusive and intimate, designing products especially 'for you.'"*[90]

Women are flocking to wellness because modern medicine doesn't take them seriously. It is sad to see that a lot of health professionals still dismiss women's experience of pain.[91]

88 Rosa Anderson-Jones, "The Future of Beauty in 2018, with Anna Moine," *Timely,* January 7, 2018.

89 Global Wellness Institute, "2018 Global Wellness Economy Monitor," accessed August 30, 2020.

90 Global Wellness Summit, "A New Feminist Wellness," 2018 Report, accessed August 30, 2020.

91 Annaliese Griffin, "Women are flocking to wellness because modern medicine still doesn't take them seriously," *Quartz,* June 15, 2017.

There is something left from a gruesome past: *"For thousands of years, women's health complaints were often diagnosed as 'female hysteria'—a catch-all term that basically implied 'it's all in her head.'"* [92]

Some facts are quite shocking: until 2016, no female mice were mandated to be part of medical studies because of systemic male bias. [93]

Women's health extends to sexual wellness, which has also been dismissed by men. It's good to see that inhibitions are falling: In fall 2017, the women's sex toy brand *Hot Octopuss* held a pop-up in New York called The Changing Room where women could get an "orgasm makeover." In two days, one thousand women attended.

APPAREL

"It is about time to acknowledge the actual size of real women's bodies. Forty percent of women globally are overweight—yet there is a lack of clothes designed to fit their needs." [94] A great female-founded company, Universal Standard, which launched in 2017, offers cool, simple garments specifically designed to flatter women sized 10–28, and the company

92   Lisa M. Lines, "The Myth of Female Hysteria and Health Disparities among Women," *RTI International*, May 9, 2018.

93   Global Wellness Summit, "A New Feminist Wellness," 2018 Report, accessed August 30, 2020.

94   Ibid.

will replace clothing for free for a year with a new size for whatever reason.[95]

When women reach menopause, their body shape evolves and the choice for clothes becomes limited: it's either designed for young bodies or for elderly women. Companies like Hope Fashion were created out of empathy for women with changing bodies, with timeless and stylish looks.[96]

The "athleisure" clothing market—athletic clothes for casual wear—was valued at $155.2 billion in 2018 and is expected to reach $257 billion by 2026. This is another exciting area for growth, as women are more and more seeking comfort in the way they dress.[97]

EMERGING OPPORTUNITIES

During our interview, my friend and business partner Cheryl Perkins, CEO of *InnovationEdge* (Business Week Top 25 Innovator in the World, CGT Visions Leader and Strategy Thought Leader) made a very astute observation: *"The 2020 COVID-19 situation revealed a few areas where women desperately need innovative solutions to better their lives. In these high-pressure times, the majority of childcare and eldercare challenges fall disproportionately on female shoulders. Many are juggling the challenge of full-time work and full-time child responsibility in 'remote' connected settings that are creating*

---

95   Universal Standard, accessed August 30, 2020.

96   Hope Fashion, accessed August 30, 2020.

97   Allied Market Research, "Report: Athleisure Market Outlook—2026," accessed August 30, 2020.

incredible pressure. What solutions can innovative companies envision that can ease the burden on women and improve the lives of the children and elders they care about?"

WHY IS THE FEMALE MARKET AN UNTAPPED OPPORTUNITY?

WE STILL LIVE IN A WORLD DESIGNED BY MEN

Caroline Criado Perez, a journalist and author, shares some juicy examples: *"One woman reported that her car's voice-command system only listened to her husband, even when he was sitting in the passenger seat."*[98]

As she graphically pictured:

We are so used to thinking of men as the default and women as a sort of niche—a variety of man.[99]

Jessica Contrera has a quite pictorial quote:

The end of 'shrink it or pink it.'[100]

---

98 Eliane Glaser, "Invisible Women by Caroline Criado Perez – a world designed for men," *The Guardian,* February 28, 2019.

99 Ritu Prasad, "Eight ways the world is not designed for women," *BBC News,* June 5, 2019.

100 Jessica Contrera, "The End Of 'Shrink It And Pink It;' A History Of Advertisers Missing The Mark With Women," *The Washington Post,"* June 9, 2016.

I reconnected with Bill Bean—a former colleague from the corporate world—when a "Congratulate Bill" message popped up on my LinkedIn account. These are always great opportunities to rekindle relationships. We caught up on our current lives, and when I mentioned INNOVEVE® and my mission, Bill laughed and said: *"One of my ex-mother-in-law's favorite phrases when interacting with products was: 'This clearly was designed by a man!'"*

This made me laugh and triggered my curiosity. I asked my friends, and even strangers, and started to gather anecdotes from women's daily lives: some hilarious, and others more serious, which prompted me to do some more research.

Eve (a fictitious woman) crystallizes the experience of lots of women—and men reporting for their wives or daughters—I interviewed, as well as my personal stories. I invite you to follow Eve as she moves through her day in a world designed by men.

This is a special day for Eve, as she took her afternoon off to run some errands. It's also a very busy day.

Eve is getting dressed to go to work. No need to elaborate, she feels obligated to wear high heels at work. As Eve cannot properly walk or drive with her high-heeled shoes, she needs to carry a pair of flats with her for the entire day.

What are Eve's options for a purse?

The logical options to complete her suit outfit are the handbag carried by hand or on the forearm, or a fancy purse to go with the high heels. Although very elegant, it's not practical at all. Most women have opted for the baggy cross-body purses that fit all their stuff. However, these are obviously not designed for the women's body, so women end up carrying them on one shoulder. Some (including me) have sustained shoulder and neck injuries from heavy purses.

I found my right shoulder—my purse shoulder—started to look lower than the left in the mirror. I also felt some pain from my neck down my right side because of the pressure. So, I got a cute and professional backpack. The back pain went away.
LISA GILLESPIE, REPORTER IN LOUISVILLE, KENTUCKY.

Eve started to wear a backpack at work. It solved her neck and shoulder pain issues and she could comfortably fit all she needed for her day. She faced some sarcastic comments from her male colleagues, as did Laura Wolf, who works at the Department of Health and Human Services in Washington, DC: *"Several men have made jokes about whether she's off to a camping trip. 'It's ridiculous to me because many men use full-sized backpacks that could actually hold camping gear.'"*[101]

Eve takes her car today as she needs it for the afternoon. We will not mention (again) that the cross-body seat belt is obviously not designed for the female body, and that the car crash tests are conducted with male dummies, putting women's lives at risk.

---

101   Olga Khazan, "Rise of the Lady Backpack," *The Atlantic*, May 3, 2019.

Eve has a packed morning with back-to-back meetings. Although the topics are different, there is one constant for the entire morning: she is freezing in all the meetings rooms. Indeed, while male and female body temperatures are similar, subtle biological variations make for a different perception, with women being comfortable at a temperature 2.5 degrees Celsius warmer than men. However, the temperature of the buildings and meeting rooms is set according to male standards.

Time for lunch. Eve is at one of her favorite "bistros" that serves family-like food, just to hear the new waiter suggesting their wonderful salad menu. Eve actually feels like having a good "steak-frites" (or if she were in France, a beautiful *"andouillette AAAAA,"* the best one!).

Looking around, she notices women pecking at their salad while men are voluptuously enjoying their steak. What is wrong with this picture? According to Paul Freedman and Chester D. Tripp, professor of history at Yale University, starting in the 1970s, kale, quinoa, and other healthy food fads were gendered as "female." Barbecue, bourbon, and "adventurous foods," on the other hand, are the domain of men. Even in the twenty-first century, echoes of cookbooks like *The Way to a Man's Heart* resound—a sign that it will take a lot more work to get rid of the fiction that some foods are for men, while others are for women.[102]

---

102 Paul Freedman and Chester D. Tripp, "How steak became manly and salads became feminine," *History News Network,* October 24, 2019.

Next is Eve's appointment for her routine mammogram. Not something Eve is looking forward to, but she takes prevention very seriously. They are running late in the facility, and Eve is in the waiting room with five other ladies, all in their not-really-sexy, faded pink gowns. Some ladies have a clearly concerned look on their face.

Suddenly, one loses it: *"If it would be for their penises, the machine wouldn't be hard, cold metal pieces squeezing their precious thing, it would be cushy velvet and feathers!"* All the women start to laugh so loudly (mainly of stress relief) that the nurse comes to inquire what is happening. When Eve fills her in on the reason of their hilarity, the nurse rolls her eyes: *"We hear that every day, but apparently it didn't make it to the device manufacturers."*

Time for Eve's reward: it's hairdresser time. She understood that the male-owned salon had a complete makeover and she is eager to see it. When she arrives, she is really impressed with the design: sleek, minimalist, contemporary. Her stylist Kareen welcomes her, and as Eve shares her first impressions, she feels Kareen is less than enthusiastic. She explains that the concrete hard floors, great for the minimalist look, are extremely uncomfortable for the feet when standing all day long. When Kareen starts to dry Eve's hair, Eve notices that the mirror in front of her begins to dance to the point that it makes her dizzy. Kareen sighs: *"Well, they thought it would be really 'cool' to have the mirrors hanging from the ceiling with flexible cables. They just didn't think that when we use the hairdryer, the hot air displaces the mirrors."*

Eve's car is overdue for replacement. She reluctantly starts to drive to the car dealership as she resents what's waiting for her, for good reasons.

Marc Somnolet, my friend and colleague we met in Chapter 4, has a wife and daughters. He heard lots of stories from them and experienced himself how bad buying a new car at a car dealership can be.

"Car buying is a system that I feel was created for men, by men, and to the purposeful exclusion of women. First of all, if I am there, the salesperson looks at me and directs the negotiation to me. The only time they will look at my wife or daughters is to ask what color they want. Because that's clearly the extent of the female decision-making in car buying!

"Second, the interaction is done in such a way that it does not allow for any empathy on either side. As the client, you certainly cannot have empathy for the person who's selling to you because you think you're going to get screwed. The person who's selling to you will ask you some personal questions, which they don't give a damn about, and they make it clearly obvious they don't really care. But they're asking because they're trying to find a further edge to create a leverage against you. And so, it throws out the whole part of empathy to start, and then it goes one step further.

"As soon as you think you've gotten somewhere, they say: hang on, I need to go speak to my manager. Right. And so, they depersonalize the thing because now you're negotiating with somebody you don't know, you've never seen, you don't even know if they actually exist, by the way. And this [sales] person

has now put themselves into the shoes of the go-between, or theoretically, they're out there for your benefit, which you know is absolutely full of shit.

"And so, to me that whole situation basically is dehumanizing. And it is one of the most god-awful systems I've ever seen in my life. So, to me it's a classic interaction that is clearly devoid of feminine characteristics."

I think Eve overheard Marc, as while driving there, she decided she was not ready for the "mansplaining" and all the "circus" around the buying process, and she decided to enjoy a great evening with her friends instead.

THERE IS A HUGE WEIGHT OF PATRIARCHAL TRADITIONS
MEN WRITE LAWS THAT AFFECT WOMEN

There's a legislative angle to the high-heel "saga:" sometimes women have no choice and need to wear high heels—for instance, in some work environments. This affects approximately one-third of women.

In 2015, Nicola Thorp, an agency receptionist, was sent home for wearing flat shoes on her first day at PricewaterhouseCoopers.[103] The same year, a group of women were turned away from a film premiere at the Cannes Film Festival in France for wearing flat shoes.[104] Even closer, in 2017 in the UK, *The*

---

103   Chris Johnston, "Woman's high-heel petition receives 100,000-plus signatures," *The Guardian,* May 12, 2016.

104   Hannah Furness, "Emily Blunt on Cannes heels row: 'everybody should wear flats,'" *The Telegraph,* May 20, 2015.

Telegraph reported that existing legislation allows women to be required to wear high heels, but only if it is considered a job requirement, and men in the same job are required to dress to an "equivalent level of smartness."[105]

What does this mean?

In Carmel-by-the-Sea, California, heels over two inches high with less than one square inch of bearing surface can be worn only with a permit. You may find this funny or think that finally somebody is trying to protect women. In fact, this is to relieve the city from any and all liability in case of accident due to the uneven nature of the terrain.[106]

THERE'S ALSO A SOCIO-CULTURAL ASPECT: THE WOMEN'S BODY IS EITHER TABOO, SHAMED, OR OBJECTIFIED

In a 2019 article, Trudy Morgan-Cole chose the picture of red stilettos for her article "Toxic Femininity." It's no coincidence: she explains how *"for generations, patriarchy has delivered very powerful messages to women:*

- *Your most important value is your physical appearance.*
- *Your most important achievement is attracting a man's attention.*
- *Other women are your competition for male attention.*

---

105 Harry Yorke, "Employers can force women to wear high heels as Government rejects campaign to ban the practice," *The Telegraph*, April 21, 2017.

106 Diane Bell, "Carmel high heel ban makes Ripley's," *The San Diego Union-Tribune*, September 10, 2014.

- *Exercising power directly—especially over men—is inappropriate: you must learn to be the 'power behind the throne.'*[107]

Are these the type of messages that contemporary women want to send and transfer to their daughters? I would rather say that we want to feel comfortable, safe, self-confident, and yes, sexy! But above all, free to make our own choices.

Here's the ultimate patriarchal origin: in high heels, women cannot easily run away from men. Somewhere it is still true today in the work environment: *"[High heels] make it harder to keep a fast pace or keep up with flat-shoed male colleagues."*[108]

Innovation that makes sense becomes irrelevant when facing social and cultural barriers. It's true in other industries like feminine hygiene.

There is still a big taboo about women's menstruation. Menstruation is considered as a dirty thing to be hidden. Until 1972, TV adverts for menstrual products were banned in the US.

There is also reluctance to use a tampon in some countries. Still in 2020, Indian girls are afraid of having anything inside their vagina before marriage.[109] In 2017, tampons accounted

---

107 Trudy Morgan-Cole, "Toxic Femininity," *Medium,* February 19, 2019.

108 Rosabeth Moss Kanter, "For International Women's Day, Think Outside the (Shoe)Box," *HBR,* March 7, 2011.

109 Anangsha Alammyan, "Will A Tampon Make Me Lose My Virginity?" *Medium,* May 27, 2020.

for just 2.9 percent of China's feminine hygiene product market, compared with 26.7 percent in the United States.[110]

This is essentially due to poor access to sex education, as well as traditional taboos regarding women's bodies. There is another layer of "biblical body-shaming:" in some cultures and religions, women who menstruate are considered "impure"

Very importantly, globally, there is the weight of the patriarchal system. In one of the surveys conducted in China, a young woman declared:

My boyfriend thinks tampons infringe on his territory, and he finds that unacceptable.[111]

What is concerning is that women support that patriarchal system. In a 2020 article, Raifa Rafiq narrates her friend's mother's negative reaction when she started using the Mooncup (a reusable cup that's placed inside the vagina to collect menstrual blood): *"I [had] never used tampons before . . . My mum was like, 'It goes inside you and messes with you. You shouldn't do that.'"* [112]

---

110 Sixth Tone, "Why Tampons Have Yet to Catch On in China," *Medium,* May 26, 2019.

111 Raifa Rafiq, "I Believed That Tampons Were Impure," *Medium,* February 7, 2020.

112 Daphne Howland, "For Nike, the future of sneaker innovation is female," *Retail Dive,* March 1, 2018.

THE FEMALE MARKET IS RIPE FOR INNOVATION

This is how Dolly Singh from Thesis Couture talks about innovation in the footwear industry:

It's this $40-billion industry, yet for eighty to one hundred years there's been almost no innovation. That's crazy.

When I looked for "high heels innovation" online, one of the first links I saw made my feet ache just looking at the shoes, not to mention the "not-so-subliminal messages." One pair of stilettos had flowers, leaves and . . . yes! Miniature teapots and teacups embroidered with small chains all over the shoe. For another pair, the heel was a kneeling naked woman lasciviously embracing a pole. No comment.

Some big players in the footwear industry start to show some renewed interest and focus on the female target. Nike claimed in 2018 that *"the future of sneaker innovation is female."* Unfortunately, they still stick to design: *"Four new ways of thinking about sneakers for women, including expanding sizes of its most popular releases, more curated retail experiences for women in stores and online, styling services for women, and more female voices in its marketing and design collaborations."*

It also seems that this direction is less driven by empathy for women's foot pain than by a commercial opportunity.[113]

---

113 Daphne Howland, "For Nike, the future of sneaker innovation is female," *Retail Dive,* March 1, 2018.

Indeed, "sell-outs of high heels declined 13.4% last year, despite a 28% increase in inventory year-on-year, while sell-outs of sneakers have risen by 38%, with a 36.6% year-over-year increase in styles."[114]

'***'

The $20+ trillion female market is an untapped business across industries, with female wellness being a key opportunity. We still live in a world designed by men and heavy with the weight of patriarchy, with men writing laws and shaming women's bodies. There is a blatant lack of empathy in designing solutions for women.

To tackle the $20+ trillion female market, we need real disruption—this will most likely come from women.

---

114 "High heel sales fall as women shift to comfort," *World Footwear*, June 22, 2018.

6

WOMEN HAVE NATURAL ADVANTAGES TO INNOVATE FOR WOMEN

---

*How many tampons does a
woman need for a week?*

This is the question male NASA engineers asked themselves in 1983 when preparing the trip for Sally Ride, the first American woman in space.

In a *New York Times* article, Jessica Bennett and Mary Robinette Kowal relate how the engineers embarked in mathematical calculations involving tables of absorbency and average flow to come up with a number of one hundred.

It was obviously not the right number, and they cut it to fifty. To Mary Robinette's point: *"If there had been any women on the team, they might have known to just ask her and then double that for redundancy.*"[115]

HOW WAS THE TAMPON BORN?

Looking at history, women didn't wait for men to innovate for their needs, but had to deal with homemade recipes, not having access to technology.

There is evidence that Egyptian women used soft papyrus tampons in the fifteenth century BCE. Roman women used wool tampons, Japanese women used paper ones, and some Asian cultures used the furry part of plants, grasses, and mosses.

However, most of the feminine hygiene and protection history has been around external pads.[116] After centuries of using homemade solutions like old rags and other pieces of fabric pinned into pants, Kotex introduced the first mass-market disposable sanitary pad in 1921; it had to be held in place by a belt. The first adhesive pad became available in 1969.[117]

In 1929 Earle Haas, a Colorado-based doctor, invented and patented the first cardboard applicator tampon. It is critical to note that the idea came from a friend of his, a Californian

---

115   Jessica Bennett and Mary Robinette Kowal, "Why NASA's First All-Women Spacewalk Made History," *The New York Times,* October 18, 2019.

116   Mary Bellis, "A Brief History of the Tampon," *ThoughtCo,* updated June 21, 2019.

117   The Museum of Menstruation and Women's Health, "Inside Mum 6," accessed September 6, 2020.

woman who told him how she was able to improvise a more comfortable and effective alternative to external pads by simply inserting a piece of sponge on the inside rather than outside.

Earle sold his patent in 1933 to a Denver businesswoman, Gertrude Tendrich, who started Tampax the same year and was the company's first president. Procter & Gamble (P&G) only acquired the brand in 1997.

During her study of female anatomy, German gynecologist Dr. Judith Esser-Mittag developed a digital-style tampon in 1945, which was made to be inserted without an applicator and just pushed in by hand. In the late 1940s, Dr. Carl Hahn, together with Heinz Mittag, worked on the mass production of this tampon called, "o.b." Dr. Hahn sold his company to Johnson and Johnson (J&J) in 1974.[118]

P&G and J&J have been the two dominant players in the market.

Throughout history, women knew what the product should be, but the tampon evolution has still been driven by men.

---

118 Funding Universe, "Johnson & Johnson History," accessed September 6, 2020.

TAMPON INNOVATION HAS BEEN LIMITED TO DESIGN AND MINOR TECHNOLOGICAL IMPROVEMENTS

It's worth wondering why you're using basically the same product as someone who was menstruating before women had the right to vote.

HANNA BROOKS OLSEN [119]

Design evolution included not-that-successful repositioning and communication, like the Kotex "rebel" tampons in neon colors and black packaging. The instructions included tips like: *"Best jeans to disguise bloating are hip huggers."*[120]

As Andrea Ayres rightfully outlines:

Never be comfortable, forget comfort. Please be concerned about what you look like at all times, even if you feel like absolute shit. Forget making yourself happy, forget doing what makes you feel good. The only thing that matters—the only thing that will ever matter—is having a small stomach.[121]

It took some courageous female entrepreneurs to tackle this challenge. Courageous takes all its meaning when it comes

---

119   Hanna Brooks Olsen, "Centuries of Period Shame Kept Us from Getting THINX Sooner," *Medium*, July 12, 2017.

120   Ibid.

121   Andrea Ayres, "Advice from my tampons," *Medium*, June 26, 2013.

to get funding, as witnessed by Julie Sygiel, founder of high-tech lingerie line Dear Kate:

I've been in front of a lot of investors; the majority of them are men," Sygiel explains, "and . . . even when sometimes a male investor is saying, 'This is an amazing concept, I understand the concept, I understand the product, but because it's not something that I would be a customer of and something that I would wear, I don't feel comfortable investing.'"[122]

It is time for women to take charge.

WHY PRODUCTS DESIGNED BY WOMEN
ARE THE NEXT BIG THING

This is the title of a 2017 *Forbes* article written by Liz Long, where she interviews Danielle Kayembe, founder of GreyFire Advisory and author of the white paper "The Silent Rise of the Female-Driven Economy."

Kayembe posits: "There is a huge, untapped potential in the market for *women-centered innovation (WCI):* products and services that are not just marketed to women, but created by them too. Women designers and entrepreneurs have an innate ability to understand the pain points and aspirations of female consumers and thus drive new types of innovation, disruption, and brand loyalty."

---

122   Hanna Brooks Olsen, "Centuries of Period Shame Kept Us from Getting THINX Sooner," *Medium,* July 12, 2017.

Every woman, by virtue of her lived expe-rience, is now a walking hub of multimil-lion-dollar business ideas.[123]

I want to specify that this chapter is not arguing that men cannot innovate for women. It is to outline that, due to their innate feminine nature and their upbringing, women have natural advantages at designing products or solutions for women.

Let's detail the reasons.

WOMEN ADDRESS THE REAL PHYSIOLOGICAL AND PSYCHOLOGICAL NEEDS OF WOMEN

SAFETY

"The FDA currently does not require tampon manufacturers to disclose ingredients, which means women could be unknow-ingly putting potentially toxic fibers into one of the most absorbent parts of their bodies." This is why women-owned companies like Conscious Period and Thinx developed tam-pons and pads that are 100 percent organic, hypoallergenic, and free of chemicals, synthetics and dyes, with some inter-esting materials like all-natural sea sponge.[124]

---

123 Liz Long, "Why Products Designed By Women Are The Next Big Thing," *Forbes*, December 22, 2017.

124 Landon Funk, "Sick Of Wasting Your Money On Tampons? Try Luna-Pads Like We Did," *Funky Feminist* (blog), accessed September 8, 2020.

AFFORDABILITY AND ACCESSIBILITY

Tampons are not cheap to start with. As a result, not all women can afford them, especially women living below the poverty line. To make matters worse, thirty-nine states tax tampons as non-necessary goods, making them even more expensive.

Several female startups have innovated new business models to address this issue.

For every purchase, Conscious Period provides biodegradable pads to homeless women in the US and will also employ these same low-income women to produce pads.

Claire Coder (a nineteen-year-old entrepreneur and founder of the Aunt Flow startup) makes a great statement:

"I didn't want to just donate money. I didn't just want to donate tampons. I wanted to find a sustainable solution for this problem." This is how she created the sustainable business plan: "Buy one, give one subscription model for tampons."[125]

COMFORT

For the humans who experience menstruation, it's quite well known that a soiled pad or a tampon or menstruation cup that's not adjusted can be extremely uncomfortable, adding to the pain of cramps.

---

125 Causeartist, "Conscious Period Created Social Impact Tampons To Provide A Healthier Option To All Women," *Medium*, July 27, 2016.

To accommodate everyone's different needs, LunaPads offers a quiz on their website that will help each individual find their perfect period product or set of products.[126]

FEELING PREPARED

I will remember that day my entire life: it was a beautiful summer day in Toulouse, South of France. I was in my 20s, enjoying drinks at a bar terrace with a male friend. I wore a white (very white!) dress. At one point, I stood up and went inside to get napkins, as we had ordered some quite greasy tapas. When I came back, my friend casually told me: "Oh, I think that you sat on a cherry!" Talk about embarrassing moments in your life. . . .

Avoiding bad surprises and being ready is part of psychological comfort.

"I loved knowing ahead of time when my period was coming and feeling prepared. With the help of my period tracking app, Clue, I knew what day my period was coming every month without fail, and I began to prepare ahead of time by taking two pain relievers a day or so before my cycle began, thanks to their reminder settings."[127]

---

126   Landon Funk, "Sick Of Wasting Your Money On Tampons? Try Luna-Pads Like We Did," *Funky Feminist* (blog), accessed September 8, 2020.

127   Anna E. Cherian, "My Experience Converting From Pills, Tampons, & Calendars to Paragard IUD, THINX, Diva Cup, & Clue," *Medium*, July 10, 2017.

Having options and backups is also part of freedom and peace of mind. Companies like LunaPads bring you free-bleeding underwear AND reusable pads AND a diva cup.[128]

EMBRACE THEMSELVES AS WOMEN
This is definitely the most significant aspect of all those innovations: address the taboo and other sociocultural barriers around menstruation.

Women like Claire Coder from Aunt Flow or Miki Agrawal, cofounder of Thinx, want to change the conversation surrounding blood and our periods.

Miki Agrawal innovated tampons with Thinx, a period panty that holds up to two tampons' worth of blood, so we can let it flow.

We've been led to think it's better to keep our blood in (and to stop it up with bleached cotton) than to let it flow naturally. But what about embracing our femininity and using technology and creativity at the service of our freedom?[129]

I love the impertinence of some initiatives that destigmatize menstruation.

Andrea Gonzalez from Girls Who Code developed the video game *Tampon Run*. In the game, players become a young

---

128 Landon Funk, "Sick Of Wasting Your Money On Tampons? Try Luna-Pads Like We Did," *Funky Feminist* (blog), accessed September 8, 2020.

129 Sophie Elmhirst, "Tampon wars: the battle to overthrow the Tampax empire," *The Guardian*, February 11, 2020.

woman who needs to collect tampons before her opponents do. When the opponents approach the player, she shoots tampons at them in self-defense. It became an overnight hit, proving the need for a lighter approach to menstruation.[130]

Petter Bragée, from the Malmö offices of Sweden's national public service broadcaster, SVT, uses humor in the video "The Period Song," where dressed-up tampons dance to a song in which we are told menstruation is "totally normal" and that it shows "the body's working as it should."[131]

In a very female sector dominated by men, it took centuries for women to finally introduce meaningful innovation addressing both basic needs like comfort or safety as well as more emotional needs like freedom and body acceptance.

It makes the point that:

Who else than a woman is better to innovate for another woman?

WOMEN START TO TAKE THEIR DESTINY INTO THEIR OWN HANDS

Coming back to high heels, we saw that legislation around high heels needed to evolve. There has been some progress. In Japan, it was fueled by a popular women's protest,

130 Girls Who Code, "Andrea Gonzales: Throwing Tampons at Gender Biases," *Medium*, February 21, 2016.

131 Christian Christensen, "We Can Learn a Lot from Dancing Swedish Tampons," *Medium*, October 21, 2015.

dubbed #KuToo (a play on *kutsu*, meaning shoes, and *kut-suu*, meaning pain in Japanese, and inspired by the #MeToo movement).[132]

Now, if any legislation is needed for high heel footwear, it should be directed toward safety:[133]

Why are high-heeled shoes still treated more as a work of art and design than as a functional product, when we know they create health problems and can even injure others? We test pills and sports gear for safety, but not stilettos. Why not?

Indeed, be it for tampons or high heels, safety is one of women's top concerns, as narrated by *The Guardian*: after 9/11, upscale New York boutiques reported a surge in demand for lower-heeled shoes: on the shop floor, they said, women were explaining they wanted shoes they could run in if necessary.[134]

WOMEN TEND TO COLLABORATE AND SUPPORT ONE ANOTHER
"Women are known for sharing products they love with other women, a behavior enhanced greatly by the use of social media—which women engage in 62% more than men."[135]

---

132   Karen Kay, "Digging their heels in: women wage war on footwear dress codes," *The Guardian,* June 8, 2019.

133   Harriet Dee, "Why we don't want to give up our heels, even though they hurt," *Medium,* November 8, 2018.

134   Jess Cartner-Morley, "Lean times and hemlines," *The Guardian,* October 31, 2008.

135   Liz Long, "Why Products Designed By Women Are The Next Big Thing," *Forbes,* December 22, 2017.

This is one of the feminine traits that will contribute to the success of a female-driven economy.

My friend Soren Kaplan is a serial innovator (Center for Effective Organizations at USC, Inc. Magazine, upBOARD, InnovationPoint, Thinkers50 Thought Leadership). While consulting with the consumer products company Kimberly Clark, he witnessed how innovation was used by the Huggies brand. Women who recently had babies were an obvious target market. Soren told me how the company recognized that these women had a kind of a deep empathy and understanding for each other. They were experiencing and seeing shared problems and issues around parenting and mothering.

Kimberly Clark decided to capitalize on that characteristic, and they created a program called "Huggies Mom-inspired" that was a kind of social community. The website became a big success in terms of brand building and became a global innovation platform where women were recognized for their creativity and innovation around baby products. Women saw it as a great vehicle for new ideas and sharing prototypes. It quickly became a business-building opportunity, as Kimberly Clark provided funding to women to advance their businesses and, in return, obtain rights to acquire the business if it went big.[136]

Sometimes women cannot do it alone, and in some countries, the nonprofits fill the gap to empower them. A great example is female-founded Pink City Rickshaw Co., an Indian

---

136 Soren Kaplan, "Mothers Of Invention: How Moms Help Huggies Innovate," *Fast Company*, August 6, 2012.

nonprofit that teaches women from Jaipur's slums how to drive electric tuk-tuks and conduct tours of the Old City. Their goal is threefold: to empower local women, improve their livelihoods, and offer an authentic experience for tourists to explore Jaipur.[137]

In the June 2nd session of the 2020 W.IN Virtual Forum (founded by Catherine Barba, entrepreneur and investor), we heard from a dynamic duo: Ann Miura-Ko, cofounder partner of Floodgate (VC firm), who backed up Danielle Li, founder & CEO of PopShop (next generation of e-commerce).

It was warming to witness their genuine bond and respect for each other as partners.

I really loved Ann's answer when asked if she invested only in women: *"We invest in the very best. . . . We didn't even notice that in the past six months it was all female; it naturally happened."*

As well as her response to the question: "What's Danielle's best quality?" *"She will do it, with or without the money."*[138]

---

137 Yana Frigelis, "What It's Like to Tour Jaipur With One of India's First Female Rickshaw Drivers," *AFAR*, Apr 9, 2018.

138 *w.in.*, "The Path Forward for Female Founders," June 16, 2020, video, 33:48.

That doesn't mean excluding men; it means excluding stereotypes.

BRIDGET BRENNAN (AUTHOR OF WHY SHE BUYS)[139]

For example, following the March 2019 debacle when NASA officials abruptly canceled the first all-female space walk outside the station because they didn't have the suits to fit both female astronauts, female designers at NASA created new inclusive spacesuits that are designed to fit more diverse bodies, including women.[140]

***

Not only do women better understand female needs, but they innovate in a practical and inventive way. They think big and try to create sustainable solutions that have a social and environmental impact. They bring the conversation to another level by including psychological needs. They are creative at developing options using new materials and business models. They don't hesitate to use technology like apps, not to forget humor, to tackle very serious issues and defy patriarchy.

---

139   New Jersey Business, "Global Female Income to Reach \$24 Trillion in 2020," *NJB Magazine,* March 6, 2020.

140   Maya Wei-Haas, "First all-woman space walk puts spotlight on spacesuit design," *National Geographic,* October 18, 2020.

Very importantly, women tend to design inclusively and eliminate stereotypes, showing that they deserve their rightful place at the innovation table.

Can they ready us for the future?

7

INNOVATING INNOVATION WITH FEMININE ENERGIES

Women will change the nature of power, rather than power changing the nature of women.

BELLA ABZUG

In French, we have two words to say power: "pouvoir" and "puissance."

The former is linked to control, command, omnipotence, domination, ascendance, and privileges (more masculine energy). It is displayed via external factors like money, belongings, and physical strength. The latter speaks to influence, competence, greatness, depth, sturdiness, and potential (more feminine energy). It comes from within and can hardly be swayed by external factors.

Some of you may be rolling your eyes and think that all this "soft" power thing is "nice to have." Let's get something straight: it works.

Before we report how it works, let me reiterate that the ultimate goal is to have all innovators—regardless of their gender—rebalance their masculine and feminine traits to round out their innovative skills. Now, we described in previous chapters the low-hanging fruit that we cannot ignore: the untapped potential of women innovators. This chapter gets deeper into some feminine energies that are precious to build our future and why now is the right time to activate them.

WOMEN DELIVER RESULTS

We rightly celebrate men's successes. It's only fair to recognize women's contributions.

WOMEN CAN BETTER SERVE CORPORATE INNOVATION

The Standard Chartered India Bank experimented with all-female employees helping female clients in two of their branches, resulting in net sales up 75 and 127 percent compared with a paltry 48 percent average among its other ninety-plus Indian branches.

"What our research shows . . . is that teams with even one woman come to feel the 'point of pain' necessary to perceive new opportunities and act on them. For companies tasked with understanding female consumers [. . .], tapping women improves the likelihood of their success by 144%."

Bottom line? Companies don't need more Boy Geniuses. To court the $20 trillion market of female consumers, companies need to get serious about leveraging female talent.[141]

It's not limited to innovating for women: "Leaders who make sure women get equal airtime are 89% more likely than non-inclusive leaders to unleash women's innovative potential. And leaders who make sure each female member on the team gets constructive and supportive feedback are 128% more likely to elicit breakthrough ideas."[142]

It is actually scientifically proven that women bring value in innovation: *"In one wide ranging study in which researchers at MIT and Carnegie Mellon sought to identify a general intelligence score for teams, they not only found that teams that included women got better results, but that the higher the proportion of women was, the better the teams did."*[143]

WOMEN ARE SUCCESSFUL ENTREPRENEURS

Women bring value to the corporate world, but where they excel—perhaps because they are tired of not being recognized in the corporate world—is in entrepreneurship.

"The feminine cares and connects with others. It empathizes and understands emotions and if there is an area in business

141 Sylvia Ann Hewlett, Melinda Marshall, and Laura Sherbin, "How Women Drive Innovation and Growth," *Harvard Business Review*, August 23, 2013.

142 Ibid.

143 Greg Satell, "Why We Need Women to Have a Larger Role in Innovation," *Inc.*, November 17, 2018.

that we seem to forget, it's care....The feminine works with oth-
ers to get the best outcomes together and knows that building
on ideas means we honour the idea itself rather than honour
the person who came up with it." [144]

Globally, more than 250 million women worldwide are entrepreneurs, according to a *Global Entrepreneurship Monitor*
Women's Report. Including the number of established busi-
nesswomen brings the total number of women entrepreneurs
to more than four hundred million worldwide.[145]

These are seventeen staggering 2019 US statistics. Here are
a few:

- There are 114 percent more women entrepreneurs than
  there were twenty years ago.
- Sixty-two percent of women entrepreneurs cite their business as their primary source of income.
- US women-owned businesses generate $1.8 trillion a year.
- Women-owned businesses added half a million jobs
  between 1997 and 2007.
- Private tech companies led by women achieve 35 percent
  higher ROI.[146]

---

144 Rebecca Livesey, "Feminine Energy Holds the Key to the Future of Entre-
     preneur Leadership," *Entrepreneur,* March 8, 2019.

145 Babson College, "More Than 250M Women Worldwide Are Entrepre-
     neurs, According to the Global Entrepreneurship Monitor Women's
     Report from Babson College and Smith College," *PR Newswire,* Novem-
     ber 18, 2019.

146 Fundera, "17 Women-Owned Business Stats You Need to Know," *Fundera,*
     accessed September 6, 2020.

WOMEN INVEST IN THE FUTURE

The masculine being more action-oriented will be more focused on the bottom line when investing. The feminine will seek to understand the longer-term impact.

An informative Survey by Merrill Lynch in partnership with Age Wave gives precious insights on women and wealth.

"When it comes to finances, women manage their wealth according to their values, goals and priorities, rather than just going for the bottom line. 77% of women say they see money in terms of what it can do for their families. As for investing, more than half (52%) of women investors are interested in or currently engaged in impact investing, generating financial returns along with social returns, compared to 41% of men.

Women are strategic in their decision-making and recognize the benefits of collaboration. Women are generally more interested in such issues as ecology, ethics and microcredit."[147]

WOMEN INVEST IN KEY AREAS FOR THE FUTURE OF HUMANITY
HEALTH

Women are starting to invest heavily in FemTech. Some investors are making great contributions to gender equality with companies like Techhammer, Pipeline Angles, Rethink Impact, SteelSky Ventures, and Halogen Ventures.[148]

---

147 Merrill Lynch, "Women & Financial Wellness: Beyond the Bottom Line," Study in partnership with Age Wave, October 25–November 22, 2017.

148 Estrella Jaramillo, "Women Investing In Femtech II: Closing the Gender Gaps in Investment and Health Innovation," *Forbes,* August 26, 2019.

The Global Wellness Summit organized a very interesting event in June 2020 to discuss the future of nutrition and healthy eating where we heard from food experts around the world. They issued a white paper on the topic, repositioning food as "Nourishment for Body, Mind, and Spirit," possibly even medicine. This was an important topic as health crises like the COVID-19 pandemic reactivated the importance of the immune system: *"Good nutrition is actually life or death."*[149]

What struck me in all the conversations and reading is how well positioned women were to reinvent the way we see food. Women are natural nurturers and the ones who usually cook for their families. Food is key to family and social connections. Communities have the power to improve food environments and food security for all, and we explored how women were especially gifted at building communities.

THE ENVIRONMENT

Sonia Smith reports about Katharine Hayhoe, a respected atmospheric scientist at Texas Tech University:

Hayhoe often likens herself to a doctor, but her patient is the planet. After taking its temperature, she feels compelled to report her diagnosis: because of man-made carbon emissions, the earth is running a fever.[150]

---

149 Global Wellness Institute, "RESETTING THE WORLD WITH WELL-NESS: Food as Nourishment for Body, Mind, and Spirit," *Global Wellness Institute*, June 3, 2020.

150 Sonia Smith, "Unfriendly Climate," *Pocket,* accessed September 6, 2020, originally appeared on Texas Monthly and was published April 15, 2016.

At the TEDWomen 2018 event, writer and environmentalist Katharine Wilkinson demonstrated *"how empowering women and girls could stop global warming."* She hit some key points:

- Women are the primary farmers of the world, producing 60 to 80 percent of food in lower-income countries with a higher productivity than men (20 to 30 percent more food).
- There is a ripple effect on forests: Project Drawdown estimates that addressing inequity in agriculture could prevent two billion tons of emissions between now and 2050.
- Finally, investing in girls' education and in family planning means better health for women and their children and better financial security for more capacity to navigate a climate-changing world.[151]

As nurturers, women bring the message to younger generations. In the last day of the 2020 W.IN Virtual Forum, Catherine Barba interviewed Miranda Massie, the director of the Climate Museum, along with three twelve-year-old kids. It was a very touching session. The level of awareness and consciousness of those kids about climate change was amazing. It gave us hope to witness this community of action.[152]

WOMEN INNOVATE WITH A PURPOSE

At the very beginning of my career, I joined the research and development department of a French company specialized

151   *TED Talks*, "Katharine Wilkinson: How empowering women and girls could stop global warming," TEDWomen 2018, video, 13:40.

152   *w.in.*, "Together for the planet, right here, right now," June 16, 2020, video, 42:23.

in home care products. As I was the youngest and last one to join the team, fresh from my PhD in chemistry, I was assigned to the "Eau de Javel" (hypochlorite bleach) product. It was considered a very basic commodity product without any interest compared to a more sophisticated floor cleaner or fabric softener formulation.

With my enthusiasm, optimism, and curious mind, I looked at it through a totally different lens: beyond a quite fascinating chemistry due to its instability, I saw an affordable global product that saved lives in the case of pandemics like cholera.

I worked in partnership with marketing and the Pasteur Institute on this facet of the product.

As a result, I traveled the world to share my knowledge, ended up live on prime-time French TV (as no marketer wanted to take the risk of a live exposure), and got an offer from Colgate-Palmolive, who was interested in my expertise in that product.

There is something to be said about looking beyond the obvious and following your heart toward a bigger purpose.

Women realize the environmental impact of the fashion industry, which produces 10 percent of all humanity's carbon emissions, and reinvent new business models:[153]

---

153   Morgan McFall-Johnsen, "The fashion industry emits more carbon than international flights and maritime shipping combined. Here are the biggest ways it impacts the planet," *Business Insider,* October 21, 2019.

- Renting clothes from companies like Rent the Runway gives you access to thousands of styles from dream designers
- Mass personalization leveraging technology and AI
- Sustainable luxury like Amall, a luxury apparel brand that takes into consideration the ethical and environmental impact of today's fashion.

WHY IS IT THE RIGHT TIME FOR FEMALE INNOVATION?

THIS WORLD NEEDS FEMININE ENERGY TO HEAL

It's been more than a decade that I have been a member of AMI, an innovation learning community that felt like family from the day I joined. When I introduced my new company INNOVEVE® to my community of friends in 2018, Sylvester Taylor, now the AMI Chair, sent me the link to a song produced by Keb' Mo' & John Lewis Parker, featuring Rosanne Cash:

Put a woman in charge.

The video is dedicated to Keb' Mo's mother, who died at the age of ninety-one. If I ever feel overwhelmed by my mission of promoting the feminine in innovation, I just need to listen to the song to smile and feel empowered.

I strongly encourage you to listen to it.[154]

---

154 *Keb' Mo'*, "Keb' Mo'—Put a Woman in Charge feat. Rosanne Cash (Official Music Video)," October 11, 2018, video, 4:04.

IN A CRISIS, WOMEN CAN REIMAGINE THINGS

Only a crisis—actual or perceived—produces real change.

MILTON FRIEDMAN

In 2020, the world had its share of crises. Health crises with the COVID-19 pandemic resulted in an economic crisis. The death of George Floyd provoked a global social unrest. If all this was not enough, there is the lurking global warming crisis. If crises are an opportunity for change, there are a lot of directions that change can take.

In her 2015 TEDx talk, "Innovation Powered by Women," MacKenzie Roebuck-Walsh outlines some characteristics of women that are key for innovation:

- Reimagine things that already are.
- Challenge the status quo.[155]

WOMEN TACKLE BIG ISSUES

Women can help address social violence, which has a specific resonance in these times of exacerbated racial issues. In her 2019 TED talk, Ivonne Roman, a police captain, demonstrates how policewomen can make communities safer: *"Less than 13 percent of police officers in the United States are women— despite their proven effectiveness in diffusing violent situations and reducing the use of force."*[156]

---

155   *TEDx Talks*, "Innovation Powered by Women | MacKenzie Roe-buck-Walsh | TEDxRapidCity," July 10, 2015, video, 6:46.

156   *TED Talks*, "Ivonne Roman: How policewomen make communities safer," TED 2019, video, 5:44.

Resilience is a key quality for innovation:

Innovative cultures elevate resilience over perfection, iteration over finality, and uncertain growth over the safety of the status quo.

CHERYL PERKINS, INNOVATIONEDGE

It's been proven that women entrepreneurs are more resilient: "Small businesses founded by women average 34% less revenue in their first year than men, says the JP Morgan Chase Institute, but remain just as viable." This is mainly due to a different approach: men will take bigger risks as they have the advantage of receiving more funding. Women will build loyalty and get longer, more recurring business from the same clients.[157]

Women are also less likely to quit their business: according to researchers at the University of Liverpool Management School, 16.3 percent of women business owners quit each year compared to 18.6 percent of men.[158]

---

157 Jared Lindzon, "Female entrepreneurs are just as resilient as men–despite lower revenue," *Fast Company,* March 1, 2019.

158 Chris Baynes, "Women entrepreneurs less likely to quit their business than men, say researchers," *Independent,* September 4, 2019.

WE NEED A FEMININE LENS IN
SCIENCE AND TECHNOLOGY

MORE DIVERSITY IS HEALTHY IN SCIENCE

We can use the continued progress of science both as aspiration during troubled times, and as a reminder of what we should be striving for: equality ... Science is a fundamentally human endeavor, and it's been encouraging to see a more diverse community get involved in science and break down pre-existing barriers.

VICTORIA JAGGARD, SCIENCE EXECUTIVE EDITOR[159]

On the first day of the 2020 W.IN Virtual Forum, Dr Miriam Merad, PhD, director of Precision Immunology Institute, Mount Sinai, reported how science is a great tool for diversity and equality and how she recognized the contribution to science from women scientists and men scientists in the same field, regardless of their sex.[160]

It reminds me of an anecdote. I was working at my PhD in an agro-chemistry laboratory in Toulouse. There was a great team of students and we all got along. Then a guy joined who was hitting on all the girls (I was an easy prey given the low number of girls in science). One day, I was in the middle of an experiment when he came behind me and whispered something really vulgar in my ear. I resisted throwing the

---

159   Victoria Jaggard, "Why science matters in a tough time," *National Geographic,* June 3, 2020.

160   *w.in.,* "Discussion with Dr Miriam Merad: Getting more women in STEM," June 16, 2020, video, 36:08.

acid that was in my beaker to his face. I put the beaker back on the bench, turned around and said very loudly so that everybody could hear: *"Jacques, you see this white lab coat? This means that I am a scientist, and scientists are like angels, they have no sex!"* He never bothered me again.

It may sound light and funny, but behind those words was a truth that Dr. Merad described more elegantly.

Science is a great tool for equality.

WE NEED A NEW ANGLE: LEARNING FROM NATURE

Biomimicry is the science of observing Mother Nature and mimicking her solutions to design innovations for human beings. One of the most famous examples is how the VEL-CRO® loop-and-hook fastener was invented by observing how the tiny hooks of the cockle-burs plant stuck to fabrics.

I was lucky enough to meet Janine Benyus, cofounder of the Biomimicry Institute, in person. It takes feminine energy to recognize nature's wisdom and learn from it instead of harvesting its resources until there are no more left.

I am delighted to share some of Janine's wisdom:

The answers to our questions are everywhere; we just need to change the lens with which we see the world. . . . What if, every time I started to invent something, I asked, 'How would nature solve this?'. . . After 3.8 billion years of research and development, failures are fossils, and what surrounds us is the secret to survival.[161]

Biomimicry is a philosophy and may take more time to develop solutions to a problem compared to other disciplines. It's not a tool you use once and forget about. One needs to take time to observe, understand and study, but the benefits are immense. It has been successfully embraced by big companies like Boeing, P&G, Patagonia, GE, and Nike.

I could be challenged here: "I can see that biomimicry has a feminine side due to its nurturing nature, but some technologies are definitely masculine." Well, not so fast, let's tackle a very male-dominated discipline.

CYBERSECURITY NEEDS FEMININE ENERGY

I was asked by a nonprofit if I could give a speech about feminine traits in cybersecurity. It was a new domain for me, so I did research and interviewed a lot of people (men and women) in the industry.

At a business social reception in New York City, I had just interviewed a young woman about cybersecurity and I was all fired up when I met a man who had his own business in that field. *"What a gift!"* I thought. I explained to him what I was trying to do, and he looked at me and said: *"Who are you to talk about cybersecurity if you don't know anything about it?"* I tried to elaborate that I was looking at it through the lens of innovation and the feminine. He interrupted: *"Let*

---

161   *AZ QUOTES*, "Janine Benyus Quotes," accessed October 12, 2020.

me explain something to you: women are good with people and men are good with computers, and cybersecurity is about computers and technology."

This time, it's not acid that almost flew to his face, but (actually good) red wine. The interview was done.

Women made up 11 percent of people in cybersecurity in 2013 and 20 percent in 2019. This is still not enough.[162] It has also been predicted that cybercrime damages will cost the world $6 trillion annually by 2021 and that there will be 3.5 million unfilled cybersecurity jobs globally by 2021.[163]

So few women in cybersecurity *"represents a real vulnerability for our country, because if we have half of the population that is largely left out of the national fight against hacks, identity theft, malware, data breaches, and other cybersecurity battle-grounds, imagine the strategic and tactical blind spots we allow to take root."*[164]

Not only do we need women to fill the gap, but women have specific skills that are precious for cybersecurity, and creativity is a most-needed skill as hackers are becoming extremely inventive, tapping into human psychology beyond technology.

---

162 *Frost & Sullivan*, "Cybersecurity in the Power Industry," July 10, 2017, accessed September 7, 2020.

163 Andrew Medal, "4 Cyber Security Risks Your Employees Must Know (and How They Can Be Prepared)," *Inc.*, October 2, 2017.

164 *Cybersecurity Ventures*, "Women Know Cyber," accessed September 7, 2020.

As women come from diverse backgrounds, not purely techni-
cal as their male counterparts, they bring a fresh approach to
cybersecurity...Unlike men, who can lose themselves in tech-
nical details, women put things into perspective and make
sure that people talk to each other, which is a more effective
approach to risk management.

JEAN-FRANÇOIS LOUÂPRE (SENIOR CYBER SECURITY
CONSULTANT AND LECTURER AT HACKENA)

'***'

Women have the power to redefine business and innovation, and they are successful at it. They have a key role to play in science and technology. We are at a critical time of crises where we need to take the right direction. Bringing all their femininity into the mix, women can help make this world a better and safer place with more compassion, collaboration, and care.

I will leave the last word to a beautiful woman:

There's nothing more predictable than
a strong woman who wants to change
things, who's brave to speak out, who's
bold in action...This is why, at eighty-one, I
cannot retire.

FORMER PRESIDENT OF LIBERIA AND NOBEL
LAUREATE H.E. ELLEN JOHNSON SIRLEAF

3

FEMININE TRAITS FOR THE INNOVATOR (REGARDLESS OF GENDER)

8

THE FEMININE
SUCCESS FORMULA
FOR INNOVATION

———

What a harmonious world! It's feminine,
this may explain why it works well.

This is the spontaneous reflection of the well-known apith-
erapist Pr. Roch Domerego admiring a beehive.[165]

Honeybees collaborate and are interdependent, relying on
each other to serve the hive. Their nursery is a model of nurturing. They constantly communicate (even if it's not verbal).
They work hard to deliver results as a joyful and loving tribe.
They are brave and generous.[166]

---

165   *13h15 le dimanche*, "Abeilles to bee or not to be," January 18, 2018, video, 45:58.

166   Jacqueline Freeman, *Song of Increase: Listening to the Wisdom of Honeybees
for Kinder Beekeeping and a Better World.* (Boulder: Sounds True, 2016), 10-11.

They exemplify what I mean by "feminine innovation;" practical innovation wrapped in love.

We have previously seen how women were more practical, instinctive, and no-nonsense when creating products and services compared to men, who look more for technology, appearance, and status. We also established that both masculine and feminine energies were needed for successful innovation.

I described in Chapter 1 how the innovation process was essentially composed of two phases: the discovery phase (also called front-end) that goes from idea to prototype, and the execution phase (also called back-end) that develops the prototype into a commercial proposition.

The feminine success formula applies to the front-end of innovation, the discovery phase, where the creativity takes place. Here there is no space for control and judgment.

From this phase depends the overall success of innovation: if it is not properly handled, the execution phase will not deliver quality innovation. To put it bluntly: "GIGO: garbage in, garbage out."

I have tapped into my thirty+ years of innovation experience and have conducted significant research to identify the feminine traits that are most critical for successful front-end innovation. Regardless of gender, any human being possesses those latent feminine traits.

It is important to first address the question: what are masculine and feminine traits? There are a lot of sociocultural studies debating this topic and it's easy to get lost. The "Feminine and Masculine Polarity Map" described in Nilama Bhat's and Raj Sisodia's book *Shakti Leadership* gives a great overview.[167]

From diverse sources, I listed the so-called "feminine" traits. I also researched the human traits that made a difference in innovation and listed a whole bunch of them, based on my experience. I compared both lists and selected the traits on specific criteria, such as their positive influence on the innovation process or their "femininity" index. I also looked at the independence and complementarity of the variables for maximum impact.

This is how I came up with the feminine success formula:

$$Em + N + I_2G \xrightarrow{Co} \heartsuit + \$$$

Let's decrypt the "chemical" formula (I obviously took some liberty with science to illustrate my point):

Em = Empathy
N = Nurturing
I = Inclusivity
I = Intuition
G = Gratitude
Co = Collaboration (catalyst)

---

167 Nilima Bhat and Raj Sisodia, *Shakti Leadership: Embracing Feminine and Masculine Power in Business,* (Oakland: Berrett-Koehler, 2016), 92.

The resulting innovation emotionally connects to consumers (the heart), bringing revenues to the business ($).

Energy like heat is needed to make some chemical reactions happen (like in cooking). Here, collaboration is the energy that allows innovation to happen by combining all the above ingredients.

Empathy is key in the understanding phase of the market and the consumer. *Nurturing* is critical for the ideation phase to grow seed ideas into bigger ones. *Inclusivity* also supports the ideation phase by contributing to the diversity of the ideas that are generated. *Intuition* helps avoid analysis paralysis in the ideas screening phase. Finally, *Gratitude* and *Collaboration* are precious in the prototyping phase, which requires teams to harmoniously work together to create a tangible product or service out of an idea.

We will detail in the coming chapters how those traits—empathy, nurturing, inclusivity, intuition, and collaboration—create innovation that emotionally connects with people and creates value for the business and the world.

Before we dive in, let's cover how we will proceed: for each feminine trait, we will start by what this trait is not, which helps us better understand what it really is. Indeed, as a student, I didn't like all the disciplines in mathematics, but I remember something that fascinated me: the "*reductio ad absurdum*," a form of reasoning used to demonstrate that a proposition is true by showing that its contrary is false. If "non-P" is false (or absurd), then "P" is true. Since those days,

I like to define something by stating by what it is not. Then we will cover why it is critical for innovation.

We will end each chapter with a "Let's Practice" section. In the context of this book, I will focus the practice on tips that help individuals—wherever they are on the gender spectrum—to become better at each feminine trait. Indeed, as we are dealing with "soft" and not "hard" skills, it is a lifelong practice that needs to be integrated into one's routine.

All six tips may not apply to you. Just pick the ones that resonate, and feel free to adapt and build on them.

Individuals will then be ready for a practice in teams applied to business: workshops and innovation services like rapid prototyping that put the feminine success formula into action.

Let's start with empathy.

9

EMPATHY

I know how you feel!

says with assurance a blond blue-eyed young boy to a (very) pregnant African American woman standing in front of him with an incredulous look on her face. This is the visual that introduces Charles Chu's article *"The ABCs of Fake Empathy."*[168]

Empathy is not sympathy, nor compassion or altruism. Where sympathy is the act of feeling *for* someone ("I am so sorry you are hurting"), empathy involves feeling *with* someone ("I feel your disappointment"). It also differs from compassion, which is a caring concern for another's suffering from a slightly greater distance and often includes a desire to help.[169]

---

168 *REDEF,* "Charles Chu: The Polymath Project: The ABCs of Fake Empathy," accessed September 8, 2020.

169 Robin Stern and Diane Divecha, "The Empathy Trap," *Psychology Today,* published May 4, 2015, last reviewed on June 15, 2016.

Empathy is the ability to feel what another person is feeling from that person's perspective.

It's often literally said that we need to put ourselves in someone else's shoes:

Walking a mile in someone else's shoes isn't as much about the walk or the shoes; it's to be able to think like they think, feel what they feel, and understand why they are who and where they are. Every step is about empathy.

TONI SORENSON[170]

This is why empathy involves active listening: *"True insight into the minds of others is not likely to come from honing your powers of intuition, but rather by learning to stop guessing about what's on the mind of another person and learning to listen instead."* [171]

A very close friend of mine who lives in France recently lost her father. I called her and caught myself in time before I almost said: "I know how you feel; I lost my dad years ago." Luckily, I am trying to practice what I preach. I bit my tongue and just listened. I asked how she was feeling, how her family was, and most importantly let her talk through it and just listened. At one point in the conversation, she is the one who

---

170 *Working a Better Life,* "Probably The Most Valuable Business Skill You Can Learn," August 9, 2019.

171 Brian Gallagher, "Taking Another Person's Perspective Doesn't Help You Understand Them," *Facts So Romantic* (blog), *Nautilus,* June 27, 2018.

said: *"Fabienne, I am sure you understand me, you lost your dad and were very attached to him."* Empathy is reciprocal.

HOW IS EMPATHY HANDLED IN THE BUSINESS WORLD?

I witnessed so many executives attending consumer focus groups to only retain what confirmed their own opinions. To me, this is "listening with interest," not "listening with empathy."

Empathy is a feeling, and most companies are not dealing very well with feelings in a business setting.

This was confirmed by Natalie Nixon, president of Figure 8 Thinking and author of *The Creativity Leap,* in our interview:

More companies are integrating empathy by applying the design thinking method, which advocates starting first from the needs of the end user. But making empathy a salient, consistent part of their business model can be challenging.

This is unfortunate, and organizations should pay more attention to empathy. Research demonstrates that empathic workplaces tend to enjoy stronger collaboration, less stress, and greater morale, all favorable conditions for innovation. CEO of Microsoft Satya Nadella shares how, over the years, he has grown to appreciate the importance of empathy in driving innovation and ensuring the products it gives rise to meet the "unmet and unarticulated" needs of its customers.

I am always searching to understand people's thoughts, feelings, and ideas. Being an empathetic father and bringing that desire to discover what is at the core, the soul, makes me a better leader.[172]

EMPATHY DOES AFFECT THE ENTIRE INNOVATION ECOSYSTEM

OUR CONSUMERS AND CUSTOMERS

Going back to my life in the corporate world, we faced the challenge of having elderly people perform good oral care. I had organized a multifunctional brainstorming session including external experts. I hired the French firm *Seniosphère Conseil,* specialized in supporting companies at creating innovation for the senior target. They had developed SOMA, a suit that simulated the accumulated effects of aging: visual and auditory loss, as well as limited mobility, especially of the hands. To develop empathy with the senior target, we asked volunteers among the participants to try the suit and perform regular oral care tasks like buying toothpaste in the store, brushing their teeth, and flossing.

I still remember the enthusiasm of a twenty-five-year-old perky female marketer who jumped on the opportunity. When she was done with the experiment, it took her a very long time to get out of the suit. She was turning her back to us and we thought she had difficulties taking if off. There was another reason, too. When she turned her face back to

---

172   Caroline Donnelly, "Microsoft CEO Satya Nadella on why empathy is essential for technology innovation," *ComputerWeekly,* October 2, 2017.

us, she was crying: *"Oh my god, I realized how much I have been bullying my grandmother, pushing her to do things and telling her she just didn't make enough efforts."* I am sure she still remembers it today and that it has changed her attitude toward elderly people.

Empathy requires that we understand the specifics of how people feel. To do this, we need to ask questions.

However, asking questions is not enough to innovate with empathy. We need to ask the right questions, and more questions, until we fully understand what the actual consumer needs are.

There is a quite famous story in the innovation world. A research company was charged to make recommendations on how to improve travelers' experience in airports. They sent a researcher who did a very thorough job exploring all parts of the airport. When in the bathroom, the researcher noticed it was full of senior people, double-checked in other bathrooms of the airport to confirm, and came back all excited to the agency: "We need to build more bathrooms in the airports and make sure they are senior-friendly."

As it was quite an investment, the agency sent another researcher. This person made the same observation but focused on the behavior and expressions of the senior people. Noticing that the elderly persons were looking up with an intense look of concentration and somewhat concern, the researcher started to ask questions, and more questions, until an older guy said: *"Well, when we are in the main hall we cannot hear the airlines' announcements as there is a lot of noise and echo. Here at least we can very clearly hear them."* Needless to say, the final recommendation from the agency was to improve the quality of the sound system, not to build more bathrooms.

This outlines the importance of fully understanding consumers to assess their actual needs before jumping to developing a solution.

I witnessed in my own life how asking the right question was critical. Innovation is my DNA and I also applied it to my career.

When I was thinking of moving from technology to marketing in the middle of my career—a true pioneer thinking at that time—I asked for input and advice. It was a quite drastic move as I was basically starting from scratch in a new discipline. All the people I talked to—mostly men—advised me against that move. According to them, I would ruin my career, losing status, income, and credibility. They were applying their own criteria without trying to understand what motivated me in this transition.

My friend Razi Imam, an innovator, serial entrepreneur, and author, denounces such an attitude in some men:

The arrogance of men to think that they have the necessary comprehension and understanding to innovate for women without truly knowing their behaviors and needs is astounding.

I had a wonderful mentor at that time, a man who was really empathetic. When I approached him for advice, he smiled.

He knew me quite well; we had traveled together for various projects. He looked at me and asked me THE question: *"Fabienne, what do you want in your career, power or fun?"* I didn't hesitate one second to answer. My mentor had observed how my life was not driven by money and control, but by love, passion, and challenges.

I ended up moving to marketing, starting from scratch as an assistant product manager. It was very tough, but I never regretted it. It was in fact one of my best initiatives in innovation!

OUR COLLEAGUES

In a lot of organizations, it is common for innovation to be attributed to a key function, usually marketing, or research and development (R&D) if this is a technology-driven company. Other functions like legal, human resources (HR), finance, and safety are often considered as "support" functions. It is unfortunate. We'll see it with *Inclusivity* and *Collaboration*; a diversity of points of view and competencies is critical for rich innovation. It all starts with having empathy for the other disciplines.

During our multifunctional experience at developing a sensorial shower gel, I remember a scientist telling a marketer: *"Oh my . . . I didn't know it was so difficult to develop a concept. To me it was just putting words on an idea".* Conversely, I smiled when I overheard another marketer sharing with a scientist who was creating a formula in our improvised laboratory: *"Wow! Next time I will think twice before asking you for a sample 'for yesterday.' I didn't understand there were so many steps and clearances to get before being able to make a simple sample."* Our safety expert also realized that the specifications asked for formula clearance were much too drastic for a prototyping exercise. Following the session, she worked with scientists to create new adapted standards.

Having empathy for others' jobs and contributions helps with team cohesion and project success.

OUR STAKEHOLDERS

Innovation can be a challenge. Among our stakeholders, our bosses and board members are often caught between a rock and a hard place, having to innovate—meaning taking risks—while reporting quarterly to Wall Street. I must admit I was the first culprit at not understanding them when I was pushing to get an innovation project approved and funded. I came to realize, though, that the best attitude was to have empathy for their struggle and work with them at finding win-win solutions.

OUR EXTERNAL PARTNERS

As the pace of technology development is accelerating, more and more large companies are partnering with start-ups to get access to novel and disruptive solutions. I worked for seven years in "external" or "open" innovation with the mission of finding new external technologies to complement our internal R&D capabilities. I know firsthand how big of a cultural shock it can be between a Fortune 500 company and a start-up with three people who developed a technology that's basically their entire company and life.

I experienced resistance from both sides. The internal scientists were upset that we had to go externally to find technologies—even fearing losing their jobs. The startup, on the other side, was very reluctant to share their technology and not to get ripped off by a big company, as it unfortunately could happen.

I had to use a lot of empathy on both sides to help them see the situation as an opportunity and not a threat.

MOTHER NATURE

Sustainability became a buzzword with the urgency of global warming, but unfortunately Mother Nature is often an afterthought in the development of new products and services. Functionality and consumer benefits are the top priority, and only when the product is successful comes the question: how can we make it more sustainable? We can do better at purposely developing innovation that respects the environment.

Having empathy for Mother Nature means incorporating her needs into the product development from the very beginning: e.g. what are the consequences of the materials choice on pollution, or of the business model on the carbon print, instead of trying to correct the situation afterwards.

IS EMPATHY FEMININE?

The controversy about the differences between the masculine and the feminine brain applies to empathy.

Scientists recognize that there seems to be a genetic component and a hormonal basis to empathy: while progesterone boosts empathy, testosterone does not.

In her book *The Female Brain,* Louann Brizendine, MD, is quite clear that women are more equipped for empathy and that this starts early in their lives. According to her, there are more "emotions mirroring" neurons in the female brain, leading to increased empathy. It gives women the capability of matching words and physical signs, looking for any incongruence and trying to interpret them. Men are less able to read facial expressions for emotions; only the appearance of tears tells them something is wrong. A study from Harvard Medical School shows that baby girls less than twenty-four hours old respond more to the distressed cries of another baby and to a human face than male newborns do.[173]

CAN EMPATHY BE ACQUIRED?

There are two areas of consensus between scientists: that gender socialization contributes to the empathic imbalance and that the brain has a great plasticity.

Men are generally encouraged to "stand up" to conflict or to withdraw when facing someone's strong feelings, not knowing how to respond without taking over or giving in. Many women are brought up to believe that empathy, in and of itself, is always appropriate, and it becomes their default mode of responding to others.

---

173   Louann Brizendine, *The Female Brain* (New York: Broadway Books, 2006).

The brain plasticity is such that we can create new connections and rewire our brains, and therefore learn new skills.

So, even if we are biologically primed for it, we have to cultivate empathy, and this could be a lifelong learning task. It needs constant practice and the right environment to know when to use it, when not to use it, and how to leverage it to get valuable insights.

LET'S PRACTICE!

These are six best practices to develop empathy for innovation. More resources, including workshops, are available on my website: www.innoveve.com.

- ☐ Talk to friends who are your target consumer
- ☐ Immerse yourself in the other person's life (ethnography)
- ☐ Travel
- ☐ Read
- ☐ Role play
- ☐ Welcome sadness.

TALK TO FRIENDS WHO ARE YOUR TARGET CONSUMER

Sometimes we go to the other side of the planet or we pay a lot of money to hear consumers talk about a specific problem—and by the way, most of the people in these focus groups tell us what we want to hear. It can be far simpler and more effective to talk to people who are in our environment and correspond to our target consumer.

The young marketer who tried the "aging suit" could have just asked her grandmother: *"How do you clean your teeth? Which products do you use? Do you have any difficulties?"* instead of "bullying" her, according to her own terms. Listening to her with an open mind and heart would have unveiled valuable insights, like that she couldn't hold the dental floss with her arthritic hands or couldn't read the claims on the toothpaste packaging in the store because the font was far too small.

IMMERSE YOURSELF IN THE OTHER PERSON'S LIFE (ETHNOGRAPHY)

Ethnography applied to business is essentially fieldwork—researchers going into the consumers' homes to better understand their practices.

The confinement due to the COVID-19 pandemic may have been a worldwide ethnographic experiment: *"We may have just unintentionally stumbled into the virtual reality training in empathy our world has needed."* In particular, dads working from home and homeschooling kids have experienced how challenging it is to juggle everything as their wives usually do. Let's just hope this experience will have changed their attitude back to work towards more gender equality instead of just getting back to "normal."[174]

---

174 Caroline Dettman, Erin Gallagher and Pamela Culpepper, "Forget returning to work as 'normal'—this is what should take its place," *Fast Company*, April 29, 2020.

TRAVEL

AFAR Editor in Chief Julia Cosgrove describes how travel can teach us empathy by starting with respecting the culture and history of every community we visit. She quotes David Mura and his book *A Stranger's Journey: Race, Identity, and Narrative Craft in Writing*: *"We are not all-knowing creatures . . . if we . . . walk into a village of strangers, we are suddenly aware that there are other ways of looking at the world; there are other ways of looking at ourselves, at who we are, at our place in the world, at the ways we identify ourselves."*[175]

Expatriation is the ultimate empathy experience in that sense. The first time I moved to the US from France, before the internet and cell phones, I experienced this feeling very profoundly. Having to "learn the ropes" of a new environment means you need to have empathy for the people and their culture and for yourself as you are discovering the extent of your strengths . . . and of your weaknesses.

Now, let's say we cannot travel far away. We can still explore our neighborhood and have a similar experience, for instance by volunteering or going to a museum. A visit at the National Museum of African American History and Culture is an example of an empathy-provoking experience.[176] I can only confirm that this museum is a jewel, informing the visitor with facts—some very cruel—while celebrating the beauty of this specific culture: yes, definitely a journey in empathy!

---

175   Julia Cosgrove, "What Travel Can Teach Us About Empathy," *AFAR*, Feb 14, 2020, from the March/April 2020 issue.

176   Ibid.

READ

When we cannot explore physically, intellectual escape is always possible, and I don't know a better way than holding a book in our hands.

Reading novels may have a positive impact of our empathy levels. According to Dr. Keith Oatley, a professor emeritus of the University of Toronto's Department of Applied Psychology and Human Development: *"When we explore the inner lives of characters on the page, we form ideas about others' emotions, motives, and beliefs, off the page."*[177]

ROLE PLAY

Back to my years in external innovation in the US: when trying to boost the shine benefit in floor cleaners, we identified a small UK company who had developed a revolutionary technology designed for another industry but that could support the benefit we were looking for. To facilitate empathy between the company owner and our scientists, I used role playing.

I divided scientists by pairs, one person playing their own role and the other person the role of the startup owner. They each had their script that the other party didn't see. Then we exchanged the roles. After a day of practice, I was amazed at the passion with which the so-called "start-up owners" were defending "their" technology and selling it to our own company. The exercise had worked like a charm, and we ended up in a successful collaboration with the start-up.

---

177 Traci Pederson, "Reading Fiction May Boost Empathy," *PsychCentral*, last updated August 8, 2018.

WELCOME SADNESS

I read John P. Weiss' Medium article because I was so intrigued by its title. It may sound odd to talk about sadness for innovation. We saw in Chapter 2 that emotions are important to create meaningful innovation. It's not limited to positive emotions, and we need to also consider the negative feelings.

John relates with humor how having a tooth extracted sparked sadness in his mind, and how "this mild melancholy fueled a lot of creative ideas." According to family therapist Betty Tullius:

Embracing sadness, on the other hand, helps us identify what is wrong and promotes thinking of ways to cope with and heal from difficult experiences. It allows us to know ourselves better and increases our empathy for others. Talking about the feeling connects us, elicits support, and brings more meaning to our relationships. We do not have to do anything to begin this process because when we experience difficulties, sadness prompts us to slow down and feel, which is exactly what we need to do to heal.

So, let's all follow John's advice: *"Go ahead, read that sad novel. Listen to that mournful song. Bawl your eyes out to that melancholy movie. Your focus will improve, you'll purge those bad feelings, and eventually emerge with a lighter heart."* And you'll be better at innovation.[178]

---

178 John P. Weiss, "This Is The Unexpected Power of Sadness" *Medium,* December 18, 2018.

`***`

Empathy is the foundational feminine trait that allows us to start the innovation process on a solid base. By deeply understanding the market's needs and the consumers' unarticulated needs, we can start to develop ideas for solutions that will address those needs. And by getting a good grasp of our innovation ecosystem—our colleagues, key stakeholders, external partners, the environment—we are in a better position to develop sustainable innovation.

10

NURTURING

—

It is easier to pluck a flower than to nurture it; which is why some would prefer to destroy your talents than nurture them.

MATSHONA DHLIWAYO[179]

Yes. It is easier to kill a nascent idea than trying to see in it the seed of a bigger idea. It's easier to ignore a challenging relationship than nurture it into a partnership. It's easier to destroy some of our innovative talents than to work hard at making them blossom. For instance, you may be very intuitive but push it back because of your education teaching you that everything has to be fact-based.

Nurturing is one of those words that I couldn't translate into French: it has a lot of equivalents, but no single word

---

179 "Nurture Quotes," *Good Reads,* accessed September 23, 2020.

translates the richness of the English word. This illustrates how many facets nurturing can have; we will try to decipher them.

NURTURING IS NOT ONLY PROTECTING

Protecting is too passive and has an element of control. It does not fit the spirit of innovation, which is about freedom, taking risks, growing, and evolving. Protecting may end up using force to finally smother what one wants to protect.

I will build on Dhliwayo's analogy. I love to garden. I am lucky enough to have an outdoor space and a green thumb. I need to protect some plants and flowers against the squirrels. I experimented with different solutions. I ended up with a combination of cat scat mats and chicken wire cloche for the most targeted items. The more effective tools like repellents (even those labeled "natural") and sturdier cloches ended up killing the plant. They either created an unfriendly environment (lack of sun and air) or even a toxic one (chemicals).

Overprotecting can kill innovation.

In an insightful 2010 TED Global talk, Steve Johnson offers to connect ideas instead of protecting them:

So in a sense, we often talk about the value of protecting intellectual property—you know, building barricades, having secretive R&D labs, patenting everything that we have so that those ideas will remain valuable, and people will be incentivized to come up with more ideas, and the culture will be more innovative. But I think there's a case to be made that we should spend at least as much time, if not more, valuing the premise of connecting ideas and not just protecting them.[180]

Of course, like for plants, a business needs some legal protection, as there are predators in that world, too. However, when it comes to innovation and ideas, I would agree that sharing and connecting bring better solutions, often quicker.

Before we move to the value of nurturing for innovation, let's define nurturing. As simply put by my friend Alain Jacques, a dear ex-colleague and great scientist, nurturing is:

Protecting, feeding, and helping to develop.

TIME IS AN ALLY FOR NURTURING INNOVATION

Nurturing innovation is very hard: *"A lot of us—me included—have been focused on instant gratification. . . . Innovation, on the other hand, lives in a very different time and place....Innovation does not live in the moment. It comes about from several years of improvement. Several years for which you might have nothing to show in return."* [181]

Some characteristics of the nurturing trait: it requires patience, perseverance, and persistence. There is a notion of independence from the thing you grow: don't "own" it; let it evolve, grow, and even be "stolen." Johnson confirms the

---

180   *TED Talks,* "Steve Johnson: Where good ideas come from," TED Global 2010, video, 17:30.

181   Ash Tapia, "Nurturing Innovation Is F*****g Hard," *Medium,* November 11, 2017.

time factor: *"A lot of important ideas have very long incubation periods."* [182]

TO NOURISH OUR BRAINS

When it comes to our health, we don't always think of nourishing our brains the way we nourish our bodies.

"Part of creativity is picking the little bubbles that come up to your conscious mind, and picking which one to let grow and which one to give access to more of your mind, and then have that translate into action." [183]

This is a great definition of nurturing: grow the "bubbles" that will eventually become innovation.

What is also precious is to nurture who we are as an innovator, our uniqueness, which is not always linked to our most glamorous side.

My mom always told me: *"What the others reproach you for, cultivate it, because it's you."* When I posted that thought on LinkedIn, somebody mentioned that the original was from Jean Cocteau: *"What the public criticizes in you, cultivate. It is you."* [184]

---

182   *TED Talks,* "Steve Johnson: Where good ideas come from," TED Global 2010, video, 17:30.

183   Nancy C. Andreasen, "Secrets of the Creative Brain," *The Atlantic,* July/August 2014 Issue.

184   "Jean Cocteau Quotes," *Good Reads,* accessed October 7, 2020.

That is great, but for me I will always hear my mom, and she was right. In the corporate world, it is customary to get annual performance evaluations. For years, I had the mention "too emotional" in the areas to improve. Until the day I attended a conference on innovation and heard a speaker say that so-called "emotional" people were in fact "passionate" people who we desperately needed for innovation. I shared this with my boss and never heard of my emotional side again.

And today, I am writing about the importance of emotions for meaningful innovation.

TO STRENGTHEN RELATIONSHIPS

Building a solid ecosystem is crucial for innovation. It starts with building relationships and nurturing them.

Women happen to be naturally more inclined to nurture. Louann Brizendine, author of *The Female Brain*, states that: *"Girls are wired for social harmony and relationships. Urge to stay connected, get approval and get nurtured... Girls' social agenda for games is to form close relationships. For boys it's the game itself, to rank, power, defensive territories and physical strength."*[185]

However, due to our brain plasticity and by creating the right environment, anyone can develop nurturing.

---

185   Louann Brizendine, *The Female Brain* (New York: Broadway Books, 2006).

TO CREATE A SAFE ENVIRONMENT

Nurturing starts with self and individual relationships, to extend to teams and the entire ecosystem.

An HHS (Health and Human Services) research article defines "nurturing environments" as follows:

"Environments that foster successful development and prevent the development of psychological and behavioral problems. . . . First, these environments minimize biologically and psychologically toxic events. Second, they teach, promote, and richly reinforce prosocial behavior. . . . Third, they monitor and limit opportunities for problem behavior. Fourth, they foster psychological flexibility—the ability to be mindful of one's thoughts and feelings and act in the service of one's values, even when one's thoughts and feelings discourage taking valued action."[186]

Let's apply this definition to innovation.

About *"minimizing biologically and psychologically toxic events."* People cannot innovate when they don't feel safe. If you feel your job or your credibility is on the line, will you venture into new risky ideas or territories? I doubt it.

"Richly reinforce prosocial behavior." In an innovation group, it is important to proactively reach out to individuals to make them feel accepted.

---

186 Anthony Biglan, Brian R. Flay, Dennis D. Embry, and Irwin N. Sandler, "The Critical Role of Nurturing Environments for Promoting Human Wellbeing," *Am Psychol.* 2012 May-Jun; 67(4): 257–271, doi: 10.1037/a0026796.

"Monitor and limit opportunities for problem behavior." One toxic person in a team can pollute the entire group. Nurturing is about trust building.

"Foster psychological flexibility—the ability to be mindful of one's thoughts and feelings." It brings it back to empathy.

I always loved bars and cafes. I must say we are lucky to have wonderful ones in France. Of course, I love my glass of wine, but more importantly, I do enjoy the "ambiance" of a bar or cafe. I always say it is like a "micro-society." There is diversity, exchange, excitement, and heated controversial discussions (especially in France). I always found this environment inspiring and stimulating.

So I was thrilled when Johnson started his TED talk with a picture of the first cafe in England and linked it to innovation: *"But the other thing that makes the coffeehouse important is the architecture of the space. It was a space where people would get together from different backgrounds, different fields of expertise, and share. It was a space, as Matt Ridley talked about, where ideas could have sex. This was their conjugal bed, in a sense; ideas would get together there. And an astonishing number of innovations from this period have a coffeehouse somewhere in their story."*

So, a nurturing environment is a: *"chaotic environment where ideas were likely to come together, where people were likely to have new, interesting, unpredictable collisions, people from different backgrounds."* [187]

187 *TED Talks,* "Steve Johnson: Where good ideas come from," TED Global 2010, video, 17:30.

This is the type of environment that companies need to create to foster innovation. Not the artificial "innovation" room full of pictures, bean bags, and coffee machines, or the open space that is supposed to encourage collaboration—research shows it doesn't—but a safe and uplifting space where people and ideas collide.

Another benefit of nurturing is pointed out by Jennifer Armbrust, author of *Proposals for the Feminine Economy*. She talks about how "nurturing cultivates abundance." The notion of abundance is key in innovation, not only for idea generation, but also for welcoming solutions from the external world, as we saw with empathy. It needs to grow organically from a group of people.[188]

TO HELP GROW IDEAS

I like how Lisa Murray defines it: "Nurturing Business Brilliance."

Nurturing is a process of incremental expansion. It's a process of allowing timing to do the work for you. It's a process of inviting your idea to show you what it can be, rather than trying to force a fit between your resources and your ideas.[189]

---

188 *Sister,* "Jennifer Armburst: Proposals for the Feminine Economy," accessed September 10, 2020.

189 Anthony Biglan, Brian R. Flay, Dennis D. Embry, and Irwin N. Sandler, "The Critical Role of Nurturing Environments for Promoting Human Wellbeing," *Am Psychol.* 2012 May-Jun; 67(4): 257–271, doi: 10.1037/a0026796.

Nurturing ideas is key for innovation efficiency: *what companies need are systems that nurture good ideas and cull bad ones—before they ever reach the decision maker's desk.*"[190]

Ideas need to adequately blossom and reach their full potential. When an idea is born in a brainstorming session or out of an innovator's brain, it is extremely fragile, like the little tender leaves of a young plant getting out of the soil. It is so easy to eliminate it or discard it. As it is not fully formed and may look weird, it's also easy to laugh at it.

In one of my workshops, I show a 2007 video of Steve Ballmer, former CEO of Microsoft. When he was asked what he thought about the iPhone, he burst out laughing: *"Five hundred dollars? Fully subsidized? With a plan? I said, 'That is the most expensive phone in the world.' And it doesn't appeal to business customers because it doesn't have a keyboard. Which makes it not a very good email machine."*[191] In February 2020, "only" 2.2 billion iPhones have been sold since production began.[192] No comment.

It can also happen that an idea is dismissed because of a bad execution. One of the worst ideas in Kickstarter is *Hitch*, a big hook that latches to your belt and drags your bags around like an awkward tail. It was obviously not very successful; however, the idea of walking hands-free in an airport

---

190 Lisa Murray, "Nurturing Business Brilliance," *Medium*, October 28, 2015.

191 *smugmacgeek*, "Ballmer Laughs at iPhone," September 18, 2007, video, 2:22.

192 Jovan Milenkovic, "How Many iPhones Have Been Sold Worldwide? – iPhone Sales Analyzed," *Kommando Tech*, February 11, 2020.

without dragging your luggage has potential.[193] Today, we see remote-control suitcases appearing in the market.[194]

This is why it is key to build the right prototypes, as we will see in Chapter 14 on collaboration.

There are a lot of other examples. Even the best innovators can dismiss a good idea based on false assumptions. The Kindle was a bold bet for Amazon, but Bezos recognized the potential ebooks had to offer. Almost no one saw it coming, though. Not even Steve Jobs:

It doesn't matter how good or bad the product is; the fact is that people don't read anymore.[195]

It is not a new phenomenon. For instance, when Alexander Fleming first published his discovery of penicillin, no one really noticed. Sometimes, the world is not ready.[196]

Another aspect is that a little idea that may be ridiculous by itself, if nurtured along with other little ideas, can lead to a big idea:

193   Michael Irving, "Eight of the worst ideas to ever cross Kickstarter," *New Atlas*, January 05, 2019.

194   *LegoTEG Creations*, "Remote Controlled Suitcase," March 24, 2018, video, 4:21.

195   *CBInsights*, "Foot In Mouth: 59 Quotes From Big Corporate Execs Who Laughed Off Disruption When It Hit," November 12, 2019.

196   Robert Gaynes, "The Discovery of Penicillin—New Insights After More Than 75 Years of Clinical Use," *Emerg Infect Dis.*, 2017 May; 23(5): 849–853, doi: 10.3201/eid2305.161556.

Creativity is the art of combining a little idea with another little idea, you may have another little idea, and so on. . . . At the end maybe a great idea will come up.

SERGE BLOCH, FRENCH ILLUSTRATOR.[197]

Computing pioneer Howard Aiken will have the last word:

Don't worry about people stealing your ideas. . . . If your ideas are any good, you'll have to ram them down people's throats.[198]

This is how tough it is to recognize a good idea from the start.

TO HELP BUILD A STARTUP OR GROW A SMALL BUSINESS
This is another phase in the innovation journey that is quite fragile.

It's not for nothing that spaces to grow start-ups are called "incubators." As per the dictionary's definition, they are places that *"provide a controlled environment for the care and protection of premature or unusually small babies."*[199]

---

197 *Special Time Edition: the Science of Creativity,* "Chapter One: The Creative Animal," August 3, 2018, 9.

198 Greg Satell, "Innovation Isn't About Ideas," *Medium,* October 6, 2018.

199 *Dictionary Online, s.v.* "*incubator,*" accessed September 10, 2020.

New businesses are extremely fragile; this is where the nurturing quality is precious.

Alexandra Fine, the cofounder of Dame Products who we met earlier in this book, has a beautiful way of expressing it in our interview:

I think growing a business feels so much like taking care of something, cleaning it up. Making sure it has what it needs to survive . . . It grows, it becomes its own little ecosystem that pulses and drives, and it becomes its own entity . . . It's like a child or like something else that you would take care of. You can't really 100 percent control it. All you can do is give it the resources. Maybe some education, whatever . . . Women tend to be a little bit more wired for nurturing and caregiving, or at the very least they're modeling, growing up with the idea that's what they're supposed to do.

In another discussion about cybersecurity, Val Rahmani (executive director, consultant, and board director with over thirty years in the technology industry) also outlined the caring facet of women for businesses:

We [women] care about the business so we don't want it to be invaded . . . It's personal; this is my company and I want it to stay safe.

LET'S PRACTICE!
The ability to nurture is certainly more natural when one's been raised by a nurturer. As we saw in Chapter 2, kids raised around women will have a tendency to pick up more

feminine traits. However, due to our brain plasticity, we can create the right environment for nurturing with some basic habits.

These are six best practices to develop nurturing for innovation. More resources, including workshops, are available on my website: www.innoveve.com.

☐ Nurture innovation in kids
☐ Care for a pet
☐ Mentor, teach, or volunteer
☐ Garden
☐ Meditate
☐ Immerse yourself in nature.

NURTURE INNOVATION IN KIDS

I am not a parent but always say that it is the most difficult job in the world. I will not elaborate on the importance of nurturing for parenting; plenty has been written on it.

I want to outline here the opportunity as parents to nurture a spirit of innovation in their kids by letting them dream, play, and just be kids. They can be your kids, or nieces or nephews, or your neighbor's kids; you can create opportunities to be around kids:

"Because innovation and creativity require nurturing at an early age, schools and parents need to encourage idealistic goals. To encourage only realistic goals serves only to create restraints to innovation. Youth often dream and imagine

huge and unreachable dreams in their future when at young ages."[200]

We are all natural innovators as kids. By nurturing this quality in their children, parents will learn from them and become better innovators.

CARE FOR A PET

Studies published by the CDC (Centers for Disease Control and Prevention) have proven the health benefits of having a pet.

They range from decreased blood pressure, cholesterol, and triglyceride to increased opportunities for exercise, outdoor activities, and socialization.[201]

Obviously, being healthy helps innovators focus their attention on innovation, but very importantly we saw how getting out of the house and meeting new people is important to get ideas. In addition, paying attention to the needs of another living creature helps develop empathy and nurturing.

---

200 Christopher Dal Porto, "Innovation Requires Nurturing," *Medium,* March 29, 2017.

201 Renee Shenton, "Q&A with Dr. Thomas J. Fogarty: How the Fogarty Institute for Innovation is nurturing breakthroughs in medical technology," *Medium,"* December 24, 2014.

MENTOR

I always encourage "reverse" mentoring. Indeed, it's easy to think the older crowd can teach things to the younger cohort, but we have so much to learn from younger people, especially in these times of accelerated technology development.

I do mentor young people in the workplace, and I get a lot out of those relationships. I also have a mentor to guide me, as entrepreneurship is new to me. I found that mentoring and being mentored at the same time was an excellent way to nurture new ideas: connect and share expertise and use those relationships as sounding boards.

Now, mentoring will work to help develop nurturing only if we take it under the angle of *"protecting"* the person from the dangers we know, *"feeding"* them with the right resources, and *"helping them develop"* their unique skills. It's certainly not about telling them what's right and wrong or telling them about your career.

GARDEN

I alluded to the fact that I find gardening very rewarding and a great way to learn patience and perseverance, which is key for nurturing as it takes time.

A story about rescuing straggling tomato seedlings and helping them grow in one's own garden, continuing to care for them even if they never reached the stage of tomato production, exemplifies how gardeners are great nurturers:

I felt it was my duty to give these wanderers a home with a chance for growth.[202]

This is how we should treat ideas: give them a chance to grow.

MEDITATE

I personally have trouble staying still to meditate, but I learned that there are no rules, as long as you reach a state of connection to yourself and to the world or to a higher purpose. I found that walking or gardening were the best ways for me to meditate.

As for gardening, the benefits of meditation are well supported. In the *Mindful Leader* blog, Steven Cohen outlines its benefits for leadership: *"Core leadership traits such as self-awareness, focus, creativity, listening, relationship development, influence, grit and having a growth mindset can be developed through meditation."*[203]

While meditation is good for creativity in general, it is especially suited to nurturing. So far, we talked about understanding and accepting others, but often we forget to take care of ourselves, particularly women: *"It's important to be gentle with ourselves and let go of guilt and self-criticism that hinders our full potential. Part of nurturing and self-care is*

---

202 Valerie Sizelove, "What Gardening Teaches You About Love," *Medium,* June 25, 2018.

203 Steven Cohen, "How Meditation Strengthens the 4 Pillars of Leadership," *Mindful Leader* (blog), October 15, 2019.

being open to support from others . . . open our minds to giving and receiving support."[204]

IMMERSE YOURSELF IN NATURE

Mother Nature is the model of nurturing, isn't she?

After all, we are nature. This is why nature grounds us. Grounding helps us be less anxious and more effective in our work and relationships. We cannot nurture ourselves and the others around us if we are anxious.[205]

According to the Global Wellness Institute, successful brands of the future will be "Nature Smart," educating consumers on the benefits of nature.[206]

I cannot say exactly how nature exerts its calming and organizing effects on our brains, but I have seen in my patients the restorative and healing powers of nature and gardens, even for those who are deeply disabled neurologically. In many cases, gardens and nature are more powerful than any medication.
NEUROLOGIST AND AUTHOR OLIVER SACKS[207]

---

204 Aytekin Tank, "Get outside: how nature can boost your health & creativity," *Jotform*, March 5, 2020.

205 Mallika Chopra, "A Meditation on Nurturing and Giving," *SONIMA*, accessed September 10, 2020.

206 Global Wellness Summit, "Successful Brands of the Future Will Be "Nature Smart"," Trendium, accessed September 10, 2020.

207 Oliver Sacks, "The healing power of gardens," *The New York Times*, April 18, 2019.

`***`

Nurturing comes into the picture to manage and grow our internal and external innovation ecosystem by nurturing our brains and our relationships. It builds trust and creates a safe environment. In that space, we can grow small ideas into bigger ones and build businesses.

11

INCLUSIVITY

———

Diversity is being invited to the party;
inclusion is being asked to dance.

VERNA MYERS[208]

You may have diversity in your innovation team, but if you don't ask each individual for their unique contribution, you will not get any benefit from that diversity.

I love how John Downer, the talent acquisition leader and HR expert I interviewed in Chapter 2, frames it:

People should think in terms of 'inclusion and diversity' as opposed to diversity and inclusion. When you first hear the term in reverse, you initially think it was said incorrectly, but this is the opportunity to educate and enlighten people to the

---

208 Janet H. Cho, ""Diversity is being invited to the party; inclusion is being asked to dance," Verna Myers tells Cleveland Bar," *Cleveland,* updated January 11, 2019; posted May 25, 2016.

difference in the two concepts, and the powerful effect that thinking about inclusion as the end goal can have on a staffing and recruiting strategy as well as with employee engagement.

INCLUSIVITY GOES BEYOND DIVERSITY

Unfortunately, "diversity and inclusion" (D&I) is often all about optics, as per this eloquent quote: *"For optics' sake, let's be sure not to announce we've hired another white guy until we find a woman of color to hire, too. Anyone have any ideas?"* [209]

A lot of companies are just trying to escape critique. For them, D&I is something to check off their corporate list. They appoint a VP of "diversity and inclusion," and if she is an African American woman, it's even better.

In a poignant blog post, Rosebell Kagumire says it all: *"I had never been showed off in a workplace to someone simply because of the colour of my skin."* [210]

Diversity focuses on the differences you see, inclusivity on the difference you can make.

Diversity is what you have, inclusion is what you do. [211]

209 Courtney Martin, "When Diversity Is Just About "Optics," It Doesn't Count," *Medium,* July 26, 2018.

210 Rosebell Kagumire, "The cost of diversity without inclusion," *Reflection and Rumination* (blog), *How Matters,* June 8, 2018.

211 Michelle Phillips and John Cigno, "Promoting Diversity, Practicing Inclusion, and Driving Positive Change in the Legal Industry," *INSIGHT Into Diversity,* July 2, 2018.

D&I SCOPE NEEDS TO EXPAND

It is often limited to ethnicity and gender. For innovation, I'd like to go beyond the "usual suspects" and talk about other differences:

- Women being more inclusive with other women and men
- Resources and sociocultural context
- Age
- Disability
- Opinions.

GENDER AND ETHNICITY

Regarding gender, I will not insist on the importance of having women in innovation as it is at the core of this book. I will look at it under a different angle: women are skilled at collaborating; however, there is some progress to be made for more inclusivity within the female global community.

Last year, I attended a women's all-day group event about diversity and inclusion. It was organized by a big company whose CEO is a woman. I noticed right away that there was a vast majority of white women but decided to keep an open mind. The morning went well, with great talks and nice bonding exercises. In the early afternoon, there was a panel of five women facilitated by the CEO, covering diversity in the workplace more specifically.

Behind me sat an Indian lady with ethnic clothes. We had already bonded during the morning break as we were joking that with our vividly colored clothes (I love colors and had a patterned shirt with bold colors), we both looked like "peacocks" in a sea of subtle pastel outfits.

In the panel Q&A session, the lady behind me took the microphone: *"I hear diversity, but I see five white ladies on stage [and she didn't mention older and quite wealthy]. I understand that the fight for equality is tough and that you may think that having to deal with ethnic women may slow you down, but I think that all together we are stronger."*

It was very well said, not aggressive but making a clear point. I was very eager to hear the CEO's reaction. I almost left the meeting when she answered: *"Well, we would have loved to have women of color but couldn't find any for this panel."*

This is exactly what men say when they don't want to promote women. Needless to say, I never came back to this group of women.

We all have something to learn from our fellow women; creativity is not linked to ethnicity. The number of businesses owned by Black women grew by 322 percent between 1997 and 2015, making them the fastest-growing group of entrepreneurs in the US.[212] According to the NWBC (National Women's Business Council): *"It was estimated that there were 1.9 million Hispanic women-owned firms in the United States*

---

212 Amy Haimerl, "The fastest-growing group of entrepreneurs in America," *Fortune*, June 29, 2015.

in 2016, employing 550,400 workers and generating $97 billion in revenues."[213]

We should learn from history. During one of my visits at the National Museum of African American History and Culture in Washington, DC, I was especially touched by the inclusivity that African American women demonstrated when they joined the national women's movement: they insisted on empowering all women regardless of their race, class, sexuality, or nationality. We should listen to them.

Women should be more inclusive when it comes to men. We as women cannot progress without our male counterparts. We must have them as allies. Recreating women-only clubs will not help, especially for innovation, where we need both the masculine and the feminine to succeed. Explaining this to men and asking them to support us as partners should be our strategy. I hope this book will help in the journey.

My inclusion is not your exclusion.

I loved that comment I heard at a Women's Association meeting I attended last year, which had true diversity, including men.

---

213   Valentina Zarya, "The fastest-growing group of entrepreneurs in the U.S.? Minority women," *Fortune,* August 21, 2015.

It boils down to the philosophical statement:

Necessity is the mother of invention.

PLATO[214]

InnoTown® is a very unusual innovation conference that happens every year in Ålesund, Norway. Their tagline, "Business NOT as usual," reflects the spirit of the conference: I like the fact that they start the conference by a welcome social gathering with drinks and food instead of offering it at the end. It definitely helps with networking! I was there in 2011 for their tenth anniversary.

Anand Giridharadas, a *New York Times* journalist and author, introduced the concepts of "hardship innovation" and what he calls "Gandhian engineering." He defines it as *"a combination of a scarcity mentality that breeds creative frugality and irreverence toward traditional ways of building a product."*

Technology 'captured' innovation, took it as hostage. It's top-down and feature-led innovation and a failure at recognizing remaining human needs.[215]

---

214 "The meaning and origin of the expression: Necessity is the mother of invention," *The Phrase Finder,* accessed September 24, 2020.

215 "Anand Giridharadas," NBC News, accessed September 87, 2020.

I witnessed this in my corporate life. I worked in different categories. Between the "oral care"—the company's flagship—and the "home care" categories, there was a difference in resources, particularly for budget (for the right strategic reasons). This is how my friend Marc Somnolet—who we already met—and his team became very creative at maximizing those resources.

A lead from the home care category was around processes. We had lots of ideas in home care, but not the resources to pursue them all, so we needed to prioritize. It was in the early 2000s that a couple of home care managers had the idea to develop a process they called "Big Hits." It was a fast-track process for some big projects that were directly submitted to senior management for a go or no-go decision. It was so efficient at accelerating decisions that it was extended to all categories.

So being inclusive of income, background, resources, and social context favors innovation.

AGE

As a baby boomer, I am especially sensitive to age discrimination. When you visualize a start-up or any innovative company, does the picture of an older woman sitting in her living room come to your mind? No such luck, it's rather a "cool" young male kid in a relaxed open work environment.

Well, as for gender, a mix in age is very favorable to innovation. In Chapter 2, we explored the brain from a gender perspective. Let's now have a look at it through an age angle.

During my years of technology scouting, I met so many interesting start-ups and small businesses. One of our potential partners was a business with a breakthrough technology led by two older men in California. I happened to travel there, and we met in person to explore the possibilities of a partnership. It was so refreshing to see those two older human beings be so enthusiastic and sharp about their business. We talked about age and innovation.

Back home in New Jersey that week, I received the book *The Secret Life of The Grown-up Brain* by Barbara Strauch. A great NPR article summarizes it:

"Scientists tell us that as we careen through middle age, our brains do slow down. We have trouble retrieving names, or we get easily distracted. . . . but Strauch details studies that suggest that the middle-aged brain is not on a steady decline, and actually improves in a number of areas as time passes. As we do things, as we learn things, the white matter increases, and the brain signals move faster. . . . and they find that the white matter peaks in middle age (40–65). Because the brain sees connections, it sees the full picture [this is why] certain studies show that an older brain can solve problems better than a younger brain."[216]

This is confirmed by recent 2019 research that shows that: *"in order to send electrical signals across brain regions, these*

---

216 NPR News staff, "The Grown-Up Brain': Sharper Than Once Thought," *NPR News*, April 20, 2010.

neurons [in the older brain] had to work harder than they would in a younger brain. It's the concept of less wiring, more firing."[217]

Three women entrepreneurs successfully launched their businesses after forty with the benefits of experience and wisdom: GB Design House took the idea of customizing weddings and grew into an all-around design studio that today produces more than a million in sales annually; Auria's Malaysian Kitchen has goods in over forty retail locations; Hidden Crown Hair is a business that sells hair extensions. Their annual revenue is projected to be in the range of eight figures, and their sales have doubled year over year.[218]

Now, do you think this "older woman sitting in her living room" has her seat at the innovation table?

DISABILITY

My husband and I recently watched a French TV broadcast that really moved us. It was about Café Joyeux in Paris ("joyeux" is "happy" in French). Café Joyeux is a hip-looking cafe on the Champs-Elysées that opened in 2018.

Café Joyeux has "a little extra": many of its cooks and waiters have one more chromosome. They are people with Down syndrome, autism, and other cognitive disabilities. French

217 Katherine Ellen Foley, "How the human brain stays young even as we age," *Quartz*, November 19, 2019.

218 Lindsay Tigar, "How these 3 women entrepreneurs launched their businesses after 40," *Fast Company*, February 28, 2019.

President Macron and his wife Brigitte came to the opening to celebrate the initiative. What struck us was the atmosphere of joy, hope, and commitment that dominated the Café's vibe. Foodie and commis chef Charles has been dreaming for years about cooking in a real restaurant:

"I'm really happy," the thirty-six-year-old with autism told AFP as he prepared gluten-free chickpea stew and osso bucco. *"I've wanted to cook for a long time, so my dream has come true. I was sick of just being a dishwasher."* [219]

Neurodiversity needs to be recognized as a competitive advantage: *"Many people with these disorders have higher-than-average abilities; research shows that some conditions, including autism and dyslexia, can bestow special skills in pattern recognition, memory, or mathematics. . . . Because neurodiverse people are wired differently from "neurotypical" people, they may bring new perspectives to a company's efforts to create or recognize value."*

I like the statement: *"Everyone is to some extent differently abled (an expression favored by many neurodiverse people)."* [220] It's like for gender as we discovered in Chapter 2: our brain is a unique mosaic with different capabilities.

---

219   AFP, "Hip cafe chain staffed by workers with Down syndrome opens in Paris," *The Local*, March 23, 2018.

220   Robert D. Austin and Gary P. Pisano, "Neurodiversity as a Competitive Advantage," *HBR,* from the May–June 2017 Issue.

When inclusivity is practiced, it gives people a safe environment where they can express their whole self, and miracles—and innovation—happen.

OPINIONS

The final aspect I want to tackle is the diversity of thinking:

Diversity of thinking is a wellspring of creativity, enhancing innovation by about 20 percent.

DELOITTE INSIGHTS[221]

Let's come back to the creation of the relaxing shower gel for which I had put together a multifunctional team that unlocked some emotional benefits via a fast prototyping process.

All team members had bought into this new exciting iterative process, with the exception of a marketing manager—let's call him Ben—who didn't want to "waste" his precious time for four days in a remote location. I could have ignored him and proceeded with the rest of the team, but I thought it was key to get his buy-in for the project. So, I met with him and convinced him to at least attend the first day.

We had a very exciting first day. The place was buzzing with activity and we were getting ready to welcome the first

---

221 Juliet Bourke and Bernadette Dillon, "The diversity and inclusion revolution: Eight powerful truths," *Deloitte Insights,* Deloitte Review, issue 22, accessed September 24, 2020.

consumers for feedback. The rule for the four days was that we all placed our smartphones in a basket in the middle of the room and didn't check them. We had special breaks to deal with the necessary calls.

In the middle of the afternoon, I saw Ben grab his phone. I quietly but firmly came to him as he was texting. He smiled and said: "Hold on, I am just texting my boss that I will stay for the four days as this is working so well and I am curious to see the outcome."

After the session, he was my best advocate in the company for the new process. It's really worth integrating people who may not be buying into what you're doing, or may even be hostile, as long as they are in the minority and don't ruin the experience.

We saw that people are more successful when they feel they can use their unique strengths and skills every day. When companies are more inclusive, their employees feel a sense of belonging, which is extremely important in building trust and productivity, creating a safe environment favorable for innovation.

Inclusivity enables a richer interdisciplinary and inter-cultural interaction. With the speed and complexity of technology development, nobody owns the truth and has all the answers. We need to rely on different experiences and talents.

LET'S PRACTICE!

These are six best practices to develop inclusivity for innovation. More resources, including workshops, are available on my website: www.innoveve.com.

☐ Encourage people to talk about themselves
☐ Storytelling
☐ Be aware of your biases—use inclusive language
☐ Play or listen to music
☐ Practice mindfulness
☐ Practice inclusive sports like Aikido.

ENCOURAGE PEOPLE TO TALK ABOUT THEMSELVES

Sometimes a team that looks homogeneous may be more diverse than you think. It is key to get to know individuals, to access their hopes and dreams. You may discover hidden talents.

I remember during a prototyping session in Mexico, I had lunch with a young marketer I had never met. As we were exchanging about our childhood dreams, we discovered that we both wanted to become interpreters.

We had consumer groups in the afternoon that needed to be translated from Spanish into English, as most team members didn't understand Spanish. The woman who was the translator got food poisoning and couldn't come. I went to the marketing person and asked her if she could fill in. She did a marvelous job, as if she were a professional. I will never forget the look of pride at the end of the day, not only on her face, but in the eyes of her colleagues who had discovered a new facet of her.

In her book *Becoming,* Michelle Obama shares how much she loves people and learning their backstories because it gives her a good understanding of who they are. She said people focus too much on statistics and not the story. In her world, the story is more about what someone's grandfather was like, and that's more important than how much money someone made or what school they went to.[222]

STORYTELLING
This is the ultimate tool for discovering another person.

The fact that storytelling became a "buzz" word (like "innovation" or "inclusion") to check off the corporate list is a pity. It is an extremely powerful tool when it comes to communication, which is needed to understand consumers and their unexpressed needs. I can witness firsthand how effective it is to create ecosystems for innovation.

In summer 2012, I was invited to speak at an innovation conference in Nice, France. My now friend Lisa Lipkin, the storyteller we met earlier, was the first speaker on the first day. I was the second speaker.

In less than an hour, Lisa transformed a "just-starting-the-conference-and-quite-inert" audience into an emotional hub:

---

222 Michelle Obama, *Becoming,* Barnes & Noble, retrieved November 18, 2018.

some people, including my neighbor in a stiff suit, had tears in their eyes at the end of the session. I was thinking that it would be a tough challenge to follow her on stage. At the same time, it was a blessing, as she inspired me to change the beginning of my speech. I was talking about innovation at Colgate-Palmolive. When the first slides appeared on the screen with the usual facts and statistics about the company, I told the audience: "Instead of boring you with numbers that you can find on our website, let me follow Lisa's lead and tell you a story about the company:

"I had just arrived in the US from France in 1992 when I had a car accident. A truck ran into my car, and it rolled over twice, but I had nothing except for a couple of bruises. I ended up in a police car. The officer was a very young guy. He told me that he would bring me to the hospital, but I refused. He then offered to bring me to my family. I had been brave so far but I lost it when I heard the word family. . . . I started to cry and articulated between two sobs: "I-have-no-family-in-the-US!" (Remember we had no cell phones or easy internet access at that time. . . .) *A little bit disoriented, the police officer asked: "So, where shall I bring you?" "I want to go to Colgate!" "You want to go to work?" "No, Colgate is my family here!"* (Needless to say, when I arrived at Colgate, they sent me directly to the hospital.)

At the end of the conference that morning, several small businesses came and told me, *"I would never have approached Colgate, as I thought it would be this big impersonal and cold organization, but your story changed my mind."* We ended up with a great innovation partnership with one of them.

This is how powerful stories are, connecting people at a universal emotional level. And yes, emotions are compatible with business.

BE AWARE OF YOUR BIASES—USE INCLUSIVE LANGUAGE

Unconscious biases are a vast topic. It is critical to be aware of them when working in an innovation team. We usually think we are inclusive, but it's not that obvious.

Two years ago, we had a problem at home with our dryer, and a technician came to look at the vent. After thorough inspection, he told me: *"Ma'am, we have a problem here. The situation is far more serious than I thought. I need to come back tomorrow with the big boss."* I was already seeing the dollar bills piling up, but oh well, it's a fire hazard; you don't want to mess with it.

The technician came back the day after with a young guy and they started to work. After a while, I went to them and asked the technician: *"I thought you told me that you would come with the big boss?"* The young guy turned to me: *"I am the big boss."*

I felt so bad that I didn't have any answer (which is quite rare with me). When they were done, I apologized to the young guy. He smiled and brushed it away, but I insisted: *"I am the one talking about inclusivity and getting rid of biases, and I cannot even practice it myself!"*

It was an excellent lesson that we need to be vigilant, as those biases are so ingrained in our brains.

It starts with using inclusive language. I am the first culprit, greeting a mixed crowd with: "Hi guys!" thinking it's cool and non-gendered, but I got some comments from ladies that it was not appropriate.

I came across this beautiful TED Talk where Poet Ali makes us realize that we speak far more languages than we may think, communicating universal experiences like love, laughter, and loneliness—feelings and thoughts that are universal. Language is defined by a *"system of communication used by a community."* This is why it's so important to develop an innovation vocabulary—not a jargon—that is common within the company and the industry.[223]

On a lighter yet very profound note, I found that the best language to use to spark innovation was: LAUGHTER!

Having fun together has always been my recipe for successful innovation. In 1994, a week after I moved from R&D in the New Jersey Technology Center to marketing in the NYC headquarters, I got a call from the VP head of the R&D department I had worked in: *"Fabienne, it's so sad around here since you left. We miss your smile, we miss the sound of your laughter through the walls; it made us joyful and more creative. And I talk for the entire department."*

It was the best compliment I could get.

---

223 *TED Talks,* "Poet Ali: The language of being human," TEDSummit 2019, video, 14:47.

PLAY OR LISTEN TO MUSIC

I already mentioned I was a member of AMI, an innovation learning community. For the spring meeting of 2017, we gathered in Los Angeles. The theme of the meeting was around jazz music and innovation. This is when I met Christian Sands, a young jazz pianist and a wonder who was very humble.

The AMI group had a beautiful discussion with him about the parallel between jazz music and innovation and how playing music prepares you for innovation.

In a jazz band, you hear from each individual player or instrument separately. The others respect the performance and build on it. Each musician is free to improvise and unleash their creativity in a safe environment.

This is a beautiful model of inclusivity: welcoming, respecting each unique contribution, and building on it to create together something new that will enchant the crowds.

Even if you are not a musician, listening to jazz and being more attentive to the roles of the different instruments and players make you more aware of the importance of inclusivity for common creation.

PRACTICE MINDFULNESS

Mindfulness is another buzzword these days, and it is a very powerful practice. To demystify mindfulness, it's just being fully in the present, in our body and mind: thoughts, feelings, and sensations. It can be experienced through simple activities like breathing, walking, yoga, or accomplishing daily tasks. There are plenty of apps to guide the practice.

Mindfulness is beneficial to a lot of disciplines like leadership and innovation.

By making us present in the moment in a non-judgmental way, "[. . .] *one is fully engaged, aware of others, not thinking excessively about themselves and accepting reality as it is at that moment.*"[224]

These are the perfect conditions for inclusivity, to accept others' contributions as they are, without judgement.

PRACTICE INCLUSIVE SPORTS LIKE AIKIDO

Practicing sports is good for health generally, and practicing collective sports can help with inclusivity. Some sports can be intimidating, requiring either great strength or flexibility. Aikido is a great discipline as it is based on energy.

Aikido does not discriminate in terms of physical strength, size or stature, gender, nationality, religion, or age; hence it is considered a highly inclusive martial art where men and women are able to practice together without many constraints.[225]

---

224 Mark Mitchnick, "Our Two Brains, Mindfulness, and Decision-Making," *Mindful Leader,* July 1, 2019.

225 Vanessa Radd, "International Women's Day: Celebrating diversity and inclusiveness in Aikido #AikidoWomen," *Medium,* March 7, 2018.

I can hear some of you arguing that you're not athletic. Well, then, practice "verbal Aikido": yield, inquire, share, and resolve to avoid arguments and embrace another person's point of view.[226]

˴✳✳✳˴

Empathy, nurturing, and inclusivity are supporting our innovation ecosystem. Let's now focus on listening and understanding what is happening inside of us with intuition.

---

226 Don Johnson, "How 'Verbal Aikido' Can Help You Avoid Stupid Arguments," *Human Parts,* September 7, 2020.

12

INTUITION

———

Three years ago, I woke up abruptly in the middle of the night and blurted out: *"Innov . . . Eve!"* My husband I had woken up asked: *"What the heck is that?"* and I just answered: *"My new company . . ."* At 3 a.m., I went online and checked the name and domain availability. INNOVEVE®, whose mission is to help the world innovate better products and services by appreciating feminine wisdom, was born.

I had the impression that this came "out of the blue," like somebody had whispered into my ear during my sleep. Was that what we call intuition?

INTUITION IS NOT HAVING A CRYSTAL BALL

Intuition is not purely and simply emotion. It is the result of accumulated knowledge.

This may be why Bruce Kasanoff, *Forbes* contributor, gives the following definition:

Intuition is the highest form of intelligence.[227]

The most critical insight comes from a research publication:

Intuition is effective when making a decision in an area where the decision maker has in-depth knowledge.[228]

John Allman, PhD, head of a laboratory at the California Institute of Technology, explains the mechanism of intuition:

"Intuition is fast, based on pattern matching. . . . Our brains are constantly comparing current experience with the past, trying to find a fit so that we can make a quick decision. When we find a match, often in a fraction of a second, our intuition boils down a lot of experience into a simple, visceral metric: I feel good about this or not. . . . It's an automatic, intelligent response to situations we've previously learned about or experienced. . . . And the more experience we gain, the more we recognize patterns and associations."[229]

227 Bruce Kasanoff, "Intuition Is The Highest Form Of Intelligence," *Forbes,* Feb 21, 2017.

228 Boston College, "Trust your gut: Intuitive decision-making based on expertise may deliver better results than analytical approach," *Science Daily,* December 20, 2012.

229 Sarah Mahoney, "How Intuitive Are You? Take This Quiz To Find Out— And See How To Sharpen Your 6th Sense," *Prevention,* September 2, 2015.

You can't connect the dots looking forward; you can only con-nect them looking backwards. So you have to trust that the dots will somehow connect in your future. You have to trust in something—your gut, destiny, life, karma, whatever. This approach has never let me down, and it has made all the difference in my life.

STEVE JOBS

SO, HOW DID INNOVEVE® HAPPEN?

As a kid, I was fascinated by a very simple physical experi-ence: you cool down a bottle of water, and when it's super-cooled but not frozen yet, you give a sharp knock on the bottle: the water instantly turns into slushy ice before your eyes. . . . It's beautiful. . . . and intriguing. There's a surprise effect; you feel like a magician although you know there is a rational explanation.

Well, this is how my company INNOVEVE® happened: an idea that crystallized in my mind with the same combination of science and magic.

Back in 2017, during my transition out of the corporate world, I was wondering what the next step should be in my career and in my life. That step had to fit my values and have a purpose and a positive impact on those around me, if not the world. As a scientist, I went through a very thorough thinking process, gathering data and information.

I worked with coaches. I interviewed more than fifty people in my personal and professional network with two objectives:

to understand what such a transition looked like and how to prepare for it, and to understand how others saw me and which ideal job they would like to see me embrace. I took self-evaluation tests. One of the most helpful exercises was to deconstruct and reconstruct my life, and I recommend an excellent workbook called *Design the Life You Love* by Ayse Birsel for more details on how to do this.[230]

In the vision board of my future, besides the expected images of intriguing travel, love, and friendship, I had words and visuals about supporting, thanking, discovering, mixes of humans and technology, of cities and nature.

When I analyzed all this information, some themes started to emerge: innovation (which is my DNA), women, joy, empathy, recognition, and disruption. All the ingredients, all the pieces of the puzzle were here, ready to be assembled into something meaningful. Then I went on with my life and let all this information settle. I did a lot of reading, continued extensive networking to enrich and expand my network, and made yoga a daily practice. It was the scientific data part.

The magic of the iced bottle happened that night of 2017, and INNOVEVE® came to life.

---

230 Ayse Birsel, *Design the Life You Love: A Step-By-Step Guide to Building a Meaningful Future*, (Berkeley: Ten Speed Press, 2015).

INTUITION SHOULD BE A KEY
ENGINE FOR INNOVATION

TO SEE OPPORTUNITIES WHERE OTHER PEOPLE DON'T
Kirsten Green is the only venture capitalist ever named to both
TIME magazine's 100 Most Influential People list and *Vanity
Fair*'s International Best-Dressed List in the same year, 2017.

In various interviews, Green describes the power of following
her gut instinct:

- How she left Wall Street because she "sensed" that e-commerce would transform the retail world
- How she believed in Dollar Shave Club: "I remember the
  tape in my head going, *I have to invest with this guy*," she
  says. "I hadn't seen the video; I hadn't seen anything else.
  I wasn't exactly turned on by the headline of *'I'm going
  to sell razors.'* But I don't remember a conversation super
  focused on razors. I felt that he 'got' the male consumer."
- How her intuitive grasp of Emily Weiss's (founder of the
  very successful brand Glossier) vision was in sharp contrast to the response Weiss and her team received from
  other venture capital firms, according to Henry Davis,
  who was president of Glossier for four years. *"Some of
  the shit we would get was, like, spectacular,"* Davis recalls.
  *"Assistants were brought into the meeting because they're
  women and understand beauty."* Some VC guys said: *"I'm
  going to give it to my wife and see what she thinks."* And I
  would leave meetings; I'd just get up and leave.[231]

---

231 *Series: Success with Moira Forbes*, "Silicon Valley Power Player Kirsten Green
On Getting Ahead With Gut Instinct," Forbes, October 24, 2019, video, 5:11.

Green exemplifies associate professor Joel Pearson's definition of intuition: *"It's all about learning to use unconscious information in your brain."* Intuition is to make decisions without the use of analytical reasoning.[232]

TO GET THE RIGHT INSIGHTS

It was the mid 1990s. I was working in corporate marketing on the dish soap category in the US. We were transitioning the range to a compact format that delivered the same number of uses in a smaller packaging with a more concentrated formula, for the same price. We had put together lots of educational materials to explain the concept, communicate the new dosage, and show the benefits, especially regarding the carbon footprint: less water, fewer packaging materials, and more efficient packing and transportation.

The transition was going very well, except in the Hispanic market, where our market share was dragging far behind the general market. When we tried to understand what was happening, the feedback we got was that the Hispanic consumer was more conservative and loved the traditional big bottle. They were also less sensitive to the ecological aspect. Something kept bothering me, though, in the back of my mind.

I had done lots of interviews with consumers of all ethnicities in this category and read numerous research reports. Something didn't click. Indeed, in addition to the environmental benefits, it was easier for consumers to carry and store the

---

232 Cari Nierenberg, "The Science of Intuition: How to Measure 'Hunches' and 'Gut Feelings,'" *Live Science*, May 20, 2016.

bottles given the smaller weight and volume. I couldn't get why the Hispanic consumers would not favorably respond to that, particularly as the main category of buyers are women, who also usually do the grocery shopping.

I shared my feeling with my colleague who was responsible for consumer insights in the Hispanic market, a young Hispanic woman herself. She told me: *"It's funny you're coming to me with this comment; I have the same discomfort with the reasons given to us. . . . Listen, I am going to Los Angeles for focus groups on another project; why don't you come along and we talk to consumers and do store checks?"* So, we did. We contacted our sales partners in the region, and for three days, we talked to dozens of women and visited so many stores, from supermarkets to mom-and-pop stores, that I couldn't see another dish soap aisle for weeks!

Our findings were quite revealing: in fact, Hispanic women were not the ones who were conservative—it was more the retailers who didn't really change their habits, kept the big bottles at eye level on the shelf, and put the concentrated format either on a lower shelf or out of reach on the highest shelf. We also found that we needed to do more demos in store versus the other media and that we needed to better adapt our educational materials to the target. The reason for not buying the concentrate was not the target's conservatism, but their lack of awareness and understanding.

We agreed on a plan with a multifunctional team and executed it. A couple of months later, the Hispanic share was at the level of the general market.

When we have feelings that are backed up by expertise, we'd better listen to our intuition to get the right insights.

TO MAKE THE RIGHT DECISIONS

In business, we are taught that every decision we make must be data driven.

This is how a lot of innovators enter the "analysis paralysis" phase, trying to digest too much data. Kasanoff quotes Gerd Gigerenzer, a director at the Max Planck Institute for Human Development: "Intuition is *'instinctively understanding what information is unimportant and can thus be discarded.'*"[233]

Defining intuition as the *"influence of non-conscious emotional information,"* scientists are now proving that intuition is precious in decision-making. Joel Pearson claims that: *"Intuition can help people make better decisions under the right circumstances. . . . The study showed that information subconsciously perceived in the brain will help with decisions if that information holds some value or extra evidence beyond what people already have in their conscious mind."*[234]

It is proven that businesses can be successful by making decisions based on feelings on top of facts. Steve Jobs was

---

233 Bruce Kasanoff, "Intuition Is The Highest Form Of Intelligence," *Forbes,* Feb 21, 2017.

234 Cari Nierenberg, "The Science of Intuition: How to Measure 'Hunches' and 'Gut Feelings'," *Live Science,* May 20, 2016.

an outspoken believer in intuition, famous for saying his number one rule of business was to *"trust your heart and your gut."*[235]

TO SPARK COLLABORATION

We will cover collaboration in Chapter 14. It is interesting to note, though, that intuition is a precursor to collaboration. Our intuition, apparently, is to cooperate with others: *"Selfish behavior comes from thinking too much, not too little."*[236]

If we follow our intuition, we will naturally collaborate with others to innovate. But if we start to analyze too much why we should be partnering, then we may end up choosing to stay safe and not risk to enter a collaboration that may have been beneficial to us.

Does it explain why women are more collaborative, as we'll see later in this book?

IS INTUITION FEMININE?

I was already challenged on the fact that intuition was not feminine. This leads in fact to a very healthy debate.

We are all intuitive, but there are sociocultural factors that can hold men back.

---

235 Aytekin Tank, "Entrepreneurial sixth sense: how intuition drives stronger decision making," *Medium*, October 5, 2018.

236 Matthew Hutson, "Selfishness Is Learned: We tend to be cooperative— unless we think too much," *Nautilus,* June 9, 2016.

Men can be very intuitive; they have the same capabilities as women. However, they may not be as used to using them. Part of it is social, something we learn: girls are more often encouraged to share their emotions, to be more receptive, to consider other people's feelings. Judith Orloff, assistant clinical professor of psychiatry at UCLA, says: *"In our culture, we view intuition as something that's warm and fuzzy, or not masculine, so men have often lost touch with those feelings. The reality is, girls are praised for being sensitive while boys are urged to be more linear in their thinking rather than listening to their feelings."*[237]

When we turn to science, we discover the research that proves intuition is a feminine skill is all based on the fact that women are better at reading facial expressions, and therefore emotions, than men.[238] I would argue that this physiological particularity explains more about empathy than intuition.

"Socially, people treat intuition like it's a dirty word, but it's actually one of the body's survival mechanisms," says Antoine Bechara, PhD, an associate professor of neurology at the University of Iowa.[239]

Culturally, intuition is also more transmitted via women. Janice Lee, author and executive editor, remembers:

237 Colleen Oakley, "The Power of Female Intuition," *WebMD*, August 12, 2012.

238 Ronald E Riggio, "Women's Intuition: Myth or Reality? It's mostly reality," *Psychology Today*, July 14, 2011.

239 Sarah Mahoney, "How Intuitive Are You? Take This Quiz To Find Out— And See How To Sharpen Your 6th Sense," *Prevention*, September 2, 2015.

"When I was a little girl, my mother taught me the Korean concept of *nunchi* (눈치). When I was older, I came across more official definitions that defined *nunchi* (a combination of the Korean words for "eye" and "measure") as an unspoken social intuition, an awareness of the feelings of those around you, or the ability to sense another person's mood. Growing up, though, I *felt* this concept more eminently."[240]

As it is opposed to data and analytical reasoning, which are considered as "serious" stuff, intuition may have been relegated to women as something "frivolous." Let's recall the history around the inability of women to handle science that we covered in Chapter 3.

So, in summary, intuition is considered a female trait not because of innate and physiological reasons as for empathy, but more by default, for sociocultural reasons.

LET'S PRACTICE!

We all have intuitive power; we just have to unleash it. These are six best practices to develop intuition for innovation. More resources, including workshops, are available on my website: www.innoveve.com.

☐ Practice yoga.
☐ Do nothing.
☐ Sleep (eight hours/night).
☐ Walk.

---

240 Janice Lee, "What Humanity Can Learn From Plants: On trees, moss, and feeling at a distance," *Medium*, May 24, 2018.

☐ Travel.

☐ Practice minimalism.

ENJOY YOGA

I will just simply share this beautiful invitation from Adriene Mishler, founder of *Yoga with Adriene*, whom I already referenced.

"As I enter a new decade of living and begin a new season, I have set intentions to re-establish a loving relationship with my intuition. . . . We are all happy and moving and breathing. We get out of our own robot way and we listen to our guts. This is the real yoga for me...Everyone is following his or her own intuition. Everyone is listening. No robots.

So, this week, I invite you to exercise the muscle of intuition. Play with this on the mat. Perhaps before a yoga video or after. Before a walk or run or after. Play with this off the mat. During your morning ritual. In a meeting at work. In an argument or moment of stress. When you get hungry.

Go off auto pilot and see what happens when you make a commitment to listen to your gut and move from there." [241]

Yoga is definitely about connecting the body and the mind. By relaxing our body, we also relax our mind and get access to those precious unconscious thoughts that are the seeds of great ideas.

---

241 Adriene Mishler, "Hello Fear," *Yoga with Adriene* (blog), accessed October 8, 2020.

DO NOTHING

Because from stillness comes lucidity.

It may sound extreme, but it is badly needed in a world where we never stop. Actually, the confinement due to the COVID-19 pandemic put some light on the benefits of "doing nothing" for productivity.

"When you're occupied in other ways, your brain is actually working in overdrive, creating new paths between unconnected areas of your brain and sparking creative thoughts. Plus, when we're relaxed, happy, and distracted, our brains release dopamine, which has been linked to creativity.

The downside of this is that you rarely bring a pen and notepad in with you to the shower. Not only that, but taking time to let your brain rest and recover 'literally makes us more creative, better at problem-solving, better at coming up with creative ideas.'"[242]

In a recent article, *The New York Times* celebrated the Dutch concept of *niksen*: just do nothing![243]

Duke University regenerative biologist Imke Kirste reports from her research: *"To her great surprise, she found that two hours of silence per day prompted cell development in the hippocampus region of the brain.*

---

242 Tony Schwartz, "Relax! You'll Be More Productive," *The New York Times*," February 9, 2013.

243 Olga Mecking, "The Case for Doing Nothing: Stop being so busy, and just do nothing. Trust us," *The New York Times,* April 29, 2019.

'We saw that silence is really helping the new generated cells to differentiate into neurons, and integrate into the system.' This is a reminder of the brain's imaginative power: on the blank sensory slate of silence, the mind can conduct its own symphonies. But it's also a reminder that even in the absence of a sensory input like sound, the brain remains active and dynamic."[244]

So, even if it is counterintuitive (intended pun), please make sure you schedule time in your day to "do nothing." As per my friend Rebecca's words: *"Old-fashioned daydreaming as you lie in the grass on your back and stare at the sky."*

SLEEP (EIGHT HOURS/NIGHT)

To those who tell me they just need less than five hours of sleep per night and can perfectly function, I repeat: no, you can't. Not only do you need more than five hours, but new research has shown that eight hours is the natural and universal amount of sleep for optimum functioning.[245]

Sleep used to be considered as a waste of time, and it was very "hip" to pretend that you were sleeping only a couple of hours per night. However, scientists have started to warn that sleep is in fact absolutely necessary to normal functioning and survival. Lots of studies have been published. Sleep

244 Daniel A. Gross, "This Is Your Brain on Silence: Contrary to popular belief, peace and quiet is all about the noise in your head," *Nautilus*, July 7, 2016.

245 Claire Maldarelli, "How many hours of sleep do you actually need? It depends on how well you want your brain to work," *Popular Science*, April 11, 2017.

suddenly became a luxury, as per the *The New York Times* article "Sleep Is the New Status Symbol."[246]

"The overriding theme is that your brain can't constantly be bombarded with information and be expected to process it," according to Dr. Carl Bazil, director of the Division of Epilepsy and Sleep at the Columbia University College of Physicians and Surgeons. *"In many ways, it's accurate to think of your waking hours as the data-collection phase of your day, while the hours you spend asleep are the time when your brain sorts and makes use of that information. Skimp on sleep, and you handicap your brain's processing power."*[247]

Remember how INNOVEVE® was born.

JUST WALK

In a very touching personal story, Gloria Liu, featured editor at *Outside,* describes how she discovered the power of simply "walking," despite being very athletic and having overlooked that mundane activity:

"While it's true that higher-intensity exercise like running or cycling can release similar neurotransmitters, walking seems more likely to produce insights and even revelations." [248]

246 Penelope Green, "Sleep Is the New Status Symbol," *The New York Times,* April 8, 2017.

247 Carlos E. Perez, "The Link Between Sleep and Deep Learning," *Medium,* May 31, 2018.

248 Gloria Liu, "Walking Is Making a Major Comeback," *Outside,* June 8, 2020.

One theory from neuroscience is that the complex nature of walking as a movement lights up various parts of your brain at the same time."[249]

The unconscious nature of walking frees up mental bandwidth.

Liu explores further: *"When I was on the phone with Dr. Rose* (Dr. Jessica Rose, director of the Motion and Gait Analysis Laboratory at Stanford University's children's hospital), *I told her that I would like to make the case that walking is innately human. Was there any biomechanical evidence for that?"* *"It's true,"* she replied, without hesitation. She explained that bipedalism—the ability to walk upright on two legs—allowed early humans to free their hands. This, in turn, gave us the ability to use and design tools, which not only spurred brain development but probably contributed to the evolution of our dexterous hands and our ability to use language. According to her:

Bipedalism is at the root of what it means to be human.[250]

If you remember from Chapter 4, what creates great innovation is our humanity, not processes. So, if walking reconnects us to our humanity, let's go for it! I used to have walking

---

249 Nicole Dean, "Stepping Up Your Creativity: Walking, Meditation, and the Creative Brain," *Brain World,* August 21, 2020.

250 Gloria Liu, "Walking Is Making a Major Comeback," *Outside,* June 8, 2020.

meetings with my innovation team, which, combined with walking outside in nature, proved to be beneficial to the team's cohesion and creativity.

TRAVEL

Travel can both help you relax and get you out of your comfort zone. These are the perfect conditions for innovation: being relaxed, as we saw, activates intuition, and challenging ourselves helps find breakthrough solutions.[251]

Travel helps you get off your autopilot mode to be more creative.

PRACTICE MINIMALISM

I can see my friend Rebecca smile here. She is a true minimalist, and we often joke that I am the opposite. I am trying, though, as I understand the benefits.

Decluttering is very popular these days, but it's mostly confined to materialistic belongings. It's a good start, though, as a clean and minimalist space helps with mind clarity. But to go deeper, it's also critical to clear your mind.

"A minimalist approach to life helps to reduce the clutter in your head that can cause you to feel like you need to recover,

---

251 Erman Misirlisoy, "Why You Write Better When You Travel," *Medium,* March 9, 2020.

delay taking action, or procrastinate due to the overwhelm you're experiencing."[252]

With less clutter in your head, you give space for your brain to connect the dots and do its magic.

'***'

We are now connected to our brains and to our innovation external ecosystem. It's time to explore what gratitude can bring to the success formula.

---

252 Tim Denning, "Choose Minimalism to Make Life Easier on Yourself," *Medium*, December 27, 2019.

13

GRATITUDE

What's Vitamin G?

The vitamin everyone should be taking.

It's gratitude.

Gratitude is not that automatic, "commercial," mechanical "thank you" smile. Mechanical is actually a good description, as you can provoke a smile mechanically since it involves muscles.

In 1862, French anatomist Duchenne de Boulogne demonstrated that "the key difference between this 'real' happy smile and a 'fake' happy smile lies in the muscles that wrap around the eyes." All smiling involves contraction of the zygomatic major muscles, which lifts the corners of the mouth. But a "Duchenne smile" is characterized by the additional contraction of the orbicularis oculi, crumpling the skin around the eyes into crows' feet."[253]

This became a topic of discussion during the COVID-19 pandemic with people wearing masks. Not being able to see others smiling, we had to learn to look at their eyes to see if they had this famous real "Duchenne" smile.

Smiles can be faked, and so can gratitude. For instance, if you thank somebody with the hope of getting more or being perceived as good person, this is closer to manipulation than gratitude. Saying (and meaning) thank you is a good start, but gratitude is much more than that.

GRATITUDE OPENS US TO THE WORLD

As defined by Dr Robert Emmons in *The Little Book of Gratitude:*

> *Gratitude is affirming the goodness in one's life and recognizing that its source lies outside the self.*[254]

It is far from being ego-centered; in fact, it's about what's happening around us. Gratitude is linked to generosity.

---

253 "Duchenne smile: A genuine smile that involves the muscles around the eyes," *New Scientist*, accessed September 13, 2020.

254 Dr Robert A. Emmons, *The Little Book of Gratitude,* (London: Octopus Books, 2016).

You may be grateful for what you receive, but what about being grateful for having an opportunity to give?

"We're used to thinking about giving as something we should do. And it is. But in thinking about it this way, we're missing out on one of the best parts of being human: that we have evolved to find joy in helping others. Let's stop thinking about giving as just this moral obligation and start thinking of it as a source of pleasure."[255]

GRATITUDE SHAPES THE RIGHT MINDSET FOR INNOVATION

When I selected the traits for my success formula as described in Chapter 8, gratitude was in competition with others, and I wanted to limit the formula to a manageable number of traits.

Although people may not see an obvious link to innovation, I decided to keep it and give it a chance, following my intuition.

IT STRENGTHENS RELATIONSHIPS

In Chapter 9 on empathy, I related how, during our multi-functional experience at developing a sensorial shower gel, the different functions discovered what it took for another function to perform their job, like for a marketer to develop a concept or a scientist to create a new formula. This had triggered empathy that turned into gratitude. Little things started to happen, like a marketer calling a scientist or

255 *TED Talks,* "Elizabeth Dunn: Helping others makes us happier—but it matters how we do it," TED2019, video, 14:21.

sending an email to thank them for having prepared the samples under short notice. Somebody in the team had the idea of buying wooden "thank you" tokens shaped like hearts. I remember the proud look of a young female scientist showing me the growing pile on her desk.

The accumulation of those small concrete gestures completely changed the atmosphere in the team by improving communication and trust. It enhanced creativity: now, if a scientist had a consumer insight or an idea for a new product, instead of holding back from fear of being mocked or having crossed the boundaries of their function, they would share it. The worst that could happen is that they would not get a token.

It's backed up by science: *"Express gratitude when you see someone doing a good job. A positive feedback loop impacts you and those around you and can ultimately shape a healthier and happier community."*[256]

Christy Curtis is the yoga and mindfulness guide we met earlier. She is a former athlete with a strong experience in education and mindfulness coaching. During our conversation, Christy shared a straightforward thought:

Gratitude can be as simple as a presence.

It reminded me of Adriene thanking us for just "showing up" on the mat for her YouTube *Yoga with Adriene* sessions.

---

256 "The power of gratitude in the workplace," *Science News,* accessed September 13, 2020.

When I was putting together teams for brainstorming sessions or specific projects like prototyping, I had to rely on people volunteering. Most of the time, it was above and beyond their job descriptions. I remember how grateful I was just for their presence.

The beauty of gratitude is that it is reciprocal, as per poet and philosopher Mark Nepo:

The original meaning of the word "appreciate" means to move forward toward what is precious. Practicing gratitude . . . reengages our aliveness—that awakens us to what is precious. Gratitude is at the heart of reciprocity; it's the atom of relationship.[257]

In Chapter 12 on inclusivity, I told the story of the young marketer who filled in for the translator who could not make it to our prototyping session in Mexico. All of us English-speaking attendees were so grateful to her for saving the session. She came to me afterwards to tell me how grateful she was for my trust in her and for having given her the opportunity to try something new.

We all celebrated together that night, which is another positive aspect of gratitude: it leads to celebration and joy.

---

257 Mark Matousek, "The One Life We're Given: A Conversation With Mark Nepo," *Psychology Today*, October 7, 2016.

IT PROMOTES CREATIVITY

Research from the University of Zurich shows that grateful people are likely to be "idea creators". . . successful with developing new and innovative ideas and reaching solutions in unconventional ways.[258]

Gratitude opens the door to . . . the power, the wisdom, the creativity of the universe.

DEEPAK CHOPRA[259]

Kids are good at innovating because they have this natural sense of wonder, the "wow" effect. They allow themselves to be surprised. As adults, only a magic show can bring that state back to us. In an insightful article, "Travel Is No Cure for the Mind," More to That describes in an entertaining way how we love traveling as we discover new experiences. They also demonstrate how the novelty fades away as we are getting used to our new environment and that it can turn into an endless search for newness that will never satisfy us. Instead, they encourage us to rediscover what they call our "Box of Daily Experience." And what helps us achieve this is gratitude.

---

258 Aytekin Tank, "How gratitude can unlock your leadership potential," *Jotform* (blog), January 3, 2020.

259 Kimberly Mikes, "What Deepak Chopra wants you to know about gratitude," *Happier* (blog), accessed September 24, 2020.

Gratitude is what allows you to feel that same sense of wonderment about your day-to-day life as you would if you were walking the streets of a faraway city.[260]

This is a very powerful tool for innovation, as it allows innovators to look at a mundane situation with a new set of eyes and discover insights that others have overlooked since they are "blasé." Observing the steps you take and why you take them while washing the dishes may give you an idea of a new solution that could make the process more effective.

Dr. Emmons, professor of psychology at UC Davis and editor-in-chief of *The Journal of Positive Psychology,* confirms this effect of gratitude that positively influences innovation:

Highly grateful people have a worldview in which everything they have and life itself is a gift—this leads to a different interpretation of experience: not taking things for granted, not getting used to positive conditions.[261]

---

260 More To That, "Travel Is No Cure for the Mind," *Medium,* March 21, 2018.

261 Alice Robb, "The Science of Gratitude Says Older Women Are Most Grateful," *The New Republic,* November 27, 2013.

IT MAKES US LOOK DIFFERENTLY AT COMPETITION

I believe that no matter what is going on in your life, if you concentrate on what you have, you will always end up having more. If you focus on what you don't have, it will never, ever be enough.

OPRAH WINFREY[262]

Dr. Emmons cites another positive effect of gratitude: *"Gratitude also serves as a stress buffer; grateful people are less likely to experience envy, anger, resentment, regret and other unpleasant states that produce stress and thwart positive emotions."*[263]

Instead of looking at competition as a threat, trying to catch up by copying, and resenting competitors being first in market, innovators should celebrate what they have as a company: their IP, technologies, diversity, global aspect, history, and the sense of belonging and of "family" that I described in the storytelling part of Chapter 11. This prompts them to innovate by leveraging the company's unique assets.

Colgate-Palmolive would never have created the "Bright Smiles, Bright Futures" program—which brings education and smiles to children in need worldwide—without realizing

---

262 "Oprah Winfrey Quotes," *Brainy Quote,* accessed September 24, 2020.

263 Alice Robb, "The Science of Gratitude Says Older Women Are Most Grateful," *The New Republic,* November 27, 2013.

the uniqueness of our caring culture, global footprint, expertise, and employees' dedication all over the world.[264]

IT HELPS DEAL WITH DRAWBACKS

Innovation is extremely challenging as it takes time, success is not guaranteed, and failures are plentiful. It takes a lot of perseverance and a positive attitude to not give up.

Even if it sounds counterintuitive, we can be grateful for negative experiences, looking at the opportunity to learn and grow. I wouldn't push it to say I was grateful for my husband's cancer. However, looking at the bright side, it brought us even closer as a couple and turned Patrick into a professional painter.

Christy Curtis, the yoga and mindfulness guide we just referenced, shared how difficult but necessary it had been for her:

"It took me a while to be grateful for bad things that happened to me. It took me a while, but it was a practice. It was a stretch. It came through loving kindness meditation to that person who did me some harm, and that was a big step. It's very healing."

By practicing gratitude and having the courage to look at the positive side of failure, innovators become more resilient and experienced:

---

264 "COLGATE BRIGHT SMILES, BRIGHT FUTURES®", *Colgate-Palmolive*, accessed September 13, 2020.

I have not failed. I've just found 10,000 ways that won't work.

THOMAS E. EDISON.[265]

IT MAKES THINGS HAPPEN

Ingrid Lindberg is a keynote speaker, customer experience officer, and CXO chief customer. She has a rich and diverse corporate career in the health industry.

She shared in our interview how during her tenure in a big health company, she suggested to create a system to actually be available to its consumers 24/7, which was a real disruption in the industry. She was told it would be costly, but she sat down with the chief operating officer and demonstrated that the math overwhelmingly favored just going 24/7. It was such a success that the COO won global awards and was touted as a very forward-thinking leader, even if it was not his idea.

Ingrid was totally fine with this. She defines gratitude as *"a level of graciousness that really has very little to do with what you do; it has to do with what you convince others to do."*

The highest form of gratitude is allowing other people to claim that win.

INGRID LINDBERG

---

265 "Thomas A. Edison Quotes," *Brainy Quote,* accessed September 24, 2020.

IS GRATITUDE FEMININE?

A gratitude survey found evidence of a gratitude gender gap: *"Women are more likely than men to express gratitude on a regular basis (52% women/44% men), feel that they have much in life to be thankful [for] (64% women/50% men), and express gratitude to a wider variety of people."*[266]

As we saw for intuition, it may be labeled more feminine because of cultural reasons, women being socially more encouraged to be grateful, while men avoid vulnerability, which makes experiencing gratitude more difficult.[267]

According to Dr Emmons: *"The science of gratitude says that older women tend to be the most grateful. Younger men are the least grateful. I don't think there is hard wiring. Gratitude is a choice that we can become better at if we deliberately cultivate it."*[268]

LET'S PRACTICE!

At the 2019 Mindful Leader Event I attended, I had the pleasure to meet Dara and Dave Feldman, cofounders of Virtues Matter, whose mission is to "uplift humanity by inspiring radical transformation in individuals, families,

---

266 Janice Kaplan, "GRATITUDE SURVEY Conducted for the John Templeton Foundation," June-October 2012, accessed September 13, 2020.

267 Summer Allen, "Do Men Have a Gratitude Problem?" *Greater Good Magazine*, August 15, 2018.

268 Alice Robb, "The Science of Gratitude Says Older Women Are Most Grateful," *The New Republic*, November 27, 2013.

organizations, and communities," based on virtues. One of them is gratitude.

They shared a beautiful and moving video from their friends at Soul Pancake, "An Experiment in Gratitude." In that video, they ask people to think of the person they are the most grateful for and to write a letter to them explaining why. Then, out of the blue, they ask them to call the person and read the letter to them. They show how the degree of happiness increases at each step.[269]

I encourage you to download Virtues Matter's app, Virtues Cards. There's a cool feature: when you shake your phone, it brings you randomly to one of the virtues. Wouldn't it be great to get "gratitude" the first time you do it?

These are six best practices to develop gratitude for innovation. More resources, including workshops, are available on my website: www.innoveve.com.

☐ Make it an everyday practice: "Everyday Thanksgiving."
☐ Keep a gratitude journal.
☐ Read *The Little Book of Gratitude* from Dr. Emmons.
☐ Thank trees.
☐ Laugh.
☐ Cook.

---

269 *SoulPancake*, "An Experiment in Gratitude | The Science of Happiness," July 11, 2013, video, 7:13.

MAKE IT AN EVERYDAY PRACTICE

I arrived in the US in May 1992. Mid-November of that year, I felt a big excitement mounting around me and understood that Thanksgiving was approaching. It was not popular in France. When somebody explained the origin and the concept to me, I immediately loved it, as one of the rare non-commercial celebrations. During that four-day weekend, I was invited to the homes of four different American families. Understanding that it is a very family-oriented event, it was very touching to me that they would invite a stranger to their table. I had a wonderful time that long weekend; it definitely contributed to my integration into my new home.

On a light note, I don't like turkey, not to mention the stuffing. I had four big turkey meals that I ate with a smile, as they were given to me from the heart and I was grateful for the welcome. You can now imagine my face when they all gave me a turkey "doggy bag!"—which was another quite new concept for me.

When I reflected on Thanksgiving later on, I wondered why it had to be a single day in the year for gratitude—as for Valentine's Day, for that matter—and don't get me started on Women's Day. I thought it would be great to have a mini daily Thanksgiving, even if it was just thinking for one minute about what made us grateful that day.

I've been practicing and find it very uplifting. I recommend doing it personally, and for your innovation project(s). You may use small incentives like the wooden thank-you hearts I described earlier.

KEEP A GRATITUDE JOURNAL

I am not a journaling person, but it is recognized as an effective way to pause and reflect.

Virtues Matter shared how John Kralik wrote a best-selling book entitled *A Simple Act of Gratitude*. He had written thank-you notes over the course of one year, which had taught him to value the good things, and had created a discipline of positive focus.[270]

I recommend again to cover both the personal and professional domains. Take five to ten minutes to write at least every other day. It should not be just a list of stuff, but also anecdotes and stories. It could include surprises: what unexpected blessings did you benefit from recently? Don't forget to include negative experiences, trying to see any positive outcome.

You may also connect to the www.seekindness.org platform cocreated by my friend Karyn Zuidinga, cofounder at Silver Start Canada. This social platform helps people notice kindness by sharing kindness stories, a great source for gratitude.

READ DR. EMMON'S BOOK

It is a very straightforward and practical little book that's very helpful. It will guide you in your gratitude journey: what is gratitude, how does it work, what are the myths around it, and, very importantly, how to practice it.[271]

---

270 John Kralik, *A Simple Act of Gratitude.* (New York: Hyperion, 2011).

271 Dr Robert A. Emmons, *The Little Book of Gratitude,* (London:Octopus Books, 2016).

THANK TREES

No, I am not a "tree hugger," but I love nature and respect its power. Among all natural species, trees have a very special place, and we should be grateful to them.

Trees can inspire us for innovation. *"Trees can teach us to listen, see, feel, live, and perceive differently."* Trees communicate among themselves; they are a network as well as a symbiotic ecosystem with fungi and animals.

"I first learned truly about the generosity of trees from my friend N.R., who reminded me, as I pressed my palm against the trunk of a huge oak tree, how trees absorb so much for us, not just carbon dioxide and other harmful gasses, but also our pain, anxiety, suffering...Always remember to express your gratitude to the tree." [272]

LAUGH

When children play (and therefore create), what's the key sound we hear?

Laughter.

Laughing is beneficial to innovation. Indeed, a happy mind is a creative and innovative mind which helps us to deal with all the situations we are facing. *"When you are*

---

272 Janice Lee, "What Humanity Can Learn From Plants: On trees, moss, and feeling at a distance," *Medium*, May 24, 2018.

laughing, you cannot think of anything else and it clears your mind." [273]

Talking about his book *Laughter Yoga*, Maran Kataria, MD, challenges us: *"Children can laugh up to 400 times in a day, but for adults this frequency drops to barely 15 times a day. Where is our laughter?"* [274]

I remember when I asked the prototyping team the reasons of the project success, a majority stated that: *"We worked very hard, but at the same time we had so much fun; we laughed a lot, and it made things easier!"*

COOK

When we cook, we are grateful to nature for giving us the fresh ingredients and to the retail chain, be it farmers' markets or supermarkets, for making them available to us.

We are grateful to the people who taught us how to cook. Back in my childhood, I remember being mesmerized by the transformation of the food during cooking—we can see the seeds of the chemist career here—glued to my grandmother or mother when they cooked. I still have and use my grandmother's cookbook (okay, it's falling apart) and my mother's handwritten recipes. I suspect she left out some tricks since it never tastes the same as I remember. Closer in time, I have

273 *TEDx Talks,* "Laugh. breathe. innovate. | Sushil Bhatia | TEDxYouth@ CCHS," October 21, 2018, video, 18:08.

274 *Laugh for no reason* (blog), *Laughter Yoga University,* accessed September 13, 2020.

warm memories—warm in all senses of the term as it was summer in Marrakech—of spending some time of my honeymoon in the kitchen with several Moroccan ladies to learn about their traditional cooking.

The best part is the gratitude you read in people's eyes when you share your cooking. I was so proud when I did my first Moroccan recipe for my husband back home. Now he is the one mastering those recipes, and I am grateful for that pleasure he gives me.

'***'

We are now equipped with the key ingredients that will make us successful at innovation. Empathy, nurturing and inclusivity helped us connect to the outside world and understand it better through different perspectives. Intuition was more introspective and taught us how to reveal our inner genius. We now know how to express gratitude that promotes creativity and helps with drawbacks, increases trust and team cohesion, and makes people spring into action.

We just need a catalyst to accelerate innovation.

14

COLLABORATION

$$Em + N + I_2G \xrightarrow{Co} \heartsuit + \$$$

Collaboration is the energy needed to make innovation happen.

I eluded earlier to one of the best trainings I had in the corporate world on partnerships and strategic alliances, given by Jan Twombly and Jeff Shuman of The Rhythm of Business consultancy. I ended up being one of the "train the trainer" instructors.

This is what I learned by teaching and practicing.

COLLABORATION IS NOT TEAMWORK
This was one of the key messages of the training. Like innovation, collaboration is currently a buzzword, and too many people pretend to collaborate when they don't. Teamwork is

about 1+1 = 2—You can be assigned to a team and just play your part. Collaboration is 1+1 = 3 or more.

As defined by the *Civil Service College*:

The key difference between the collaboration and teamwork is that whilst teamwork combines the individual efforts of all team members to achieve a goal, people working collaboratively complete a project collectively.[275]

Collaboration, as precisely described by Jan and Jeff, is *intentional* and creates *interdependency.* How many times were you assigned to a team without wanting to be there? You're a professional and do your part. But there is not this personal commitment, this passion that makes you want to do it.

This is why I always built my one-time project teams by making sure people wanted to be part of the adventure.

In a team, you can also independently bring your expertise to the project without the help of others. In a collaboration, you need the other partners to succeed *together.*

In addition, the *Civil Service College* made an excellent point around hierarchy: *"Those collaborating work together as equals, usually without a leader, to come up with ideas or make decisions together to complete a goal. Whereas teamwork is usually overseen by a team leader, and those within a*

---

275   "Understanding the differences between collaboration and teamwork," *Civil Service College,* August, 30, 2018, accessed September 13, 2020.

team are delegated individual tasks to complete to contribute towards the team's end goal." [276]

Innovators don't do well with too much control and micro-managing. Freedom and the opportunity to take initiatives are paramount. The group self-regulates with the guidance of a facilitator. It takes more time to make decisions and move forward, but the outcome is far more sustainable.

Work by Nielsen shows that ideas developed by groups of three or more people have 156 percent greater appeal with consumers than those developed by groups where just one or two people have played a hands-on role.[277]

Can you have too much collaboration?

Aytekin Tank, founder of *Jotform,* describes the benefits of collaboration in his company. He also warns us about the downsides of too much collaboration: *"Collaborations can be unproductive, time-wasting, and a strain on top employees. . . . Over time, the best collaborators face increasing demands."*[278]

I totally witnessed that phenomenon in the corporate world. At one point, any issue was to be solved by putting so-called

276 "Understanding the differences between collaboration and teamwork," *Civil Service College,* August, 30, 2018, accessed September 13, 2020

277 Kenneth Matos, "How fostering collaboration can boost innovation," (blog), *Culture Amp,* accessed September 13, 2020.

278 Aytekin Tank, "A guide to effective (not excessive) collaboration," *Medium,* April 1, 2019.

"swat teams" together to collaborate. Employees were constantly "nominated" to be part of teams on top of their regular jobs. It happened that some individuals became very popular and "go-to" people to the point that they got burned out and totally demotivated.

Like in everything, there is a balance to reach for maximum efficiency.

WHAT ARE THE IDEAL CONDITIONS FOR COLLABORATION?

During my career I experimented with collaboration in different environments and did some research. A great inspiration came from a fellow member of AMI (the innovation learning community I already introduced), Rolf Smith. When we exchanged on collaboration for innovation, he shared what he had done when he was in the army with the so-called "hot groups."

Hot groups are seen in any institution: social institutes, academia, industry, politics.

A hot group is defined as: *"a lively, high-achieving, dedicated group, usually small, whose members are turned on to an exciting and challenging task. Hot groups, while they last, completely captivate their members, occupying their hearts and minds to the exclusion of almost everything else. They do great things fast."*[279]

279 Harold J. Leavitt and Jean Lipman-Blumen, "Hot Groups," *HBR,* from the July–August 1995 issue.

We already met my friend and partner Kaylie Dugan, the rapid prototyping process expert. Working together, we found similar conditions that favor the success of collaboration. These conditions are:

DIVERSE, SMALL, AND PASSIONATE GROUPS

Beyond the internal team, inviting external experts in a field that is related but not too close to the project is essential to stimulate creativity. For instance, in our sensorial shower gel project, we had invited a chef for the "gourmand" aspect.

Cocreation with consumers is what will accelerate the process.

Big groups can be too challenging to manage. We found a sweet spot between eight and twenty, depending on project scope.

It is not recommended to appoint people to such a group. People should want to join the group following their passion; it's a demanding endeavor.

CLEAR VISION AND ROLES

To respect the notion of interdependency that characterizes collaboration, people need to be aligned, not only on the project mission and their own role and responsibilities, but also on those of all others.

According to McKinsey:

Ninety-seven percent of employees and executives believe lack of alignment within a team impacts the outcome of a task or project.[280]

NEUTRAL, REMOTE LOCATION

Holding the key working sessions in a corporate environment does not work. The sessions last for three to four days, and people need to be fully focused, without distraction coming from the workplace or home. It doesn't need to be a fancy place. It needs to have the basic comfort and amenities to perform the job and be inspiring by its unfamiliarity.

TIME PRESSURE

When people are working together toward a common goal with a limited amount of time, it unleashes their creativity. Being time-pressed, participants do not have the luxury of overanalyzing and asking for more data; they have to follow their intuition.

HAVE FUN TOGETHER

It is absolutely critical to enjoy the time spent together. I remember evenings at the bar until midnight after the consumer groups, debriefing about the day, capturing learning, preparing the next day, and above all playing games, talking about our personal lives, and just laughing. This created solid relationships based on trust.

---

280 Editorial team, "21 Collaboration Statistics that Show the Power of Teamwork," *BIT.AI* (blog), September 2019.

Now that we know how to create collaborative conditions, let's understand what collaboration brings to innovation.

HOW DOES COLLABORATION CATALYZE INNOVATION?

Besides being the "glue" that gives cohesion to groups, collaboration is also precious in some specific aspects.

GETS THE RIGHT INSIGHTS

We already met Alexandra Fine, founder of Dame Products, which creates products and devices for female sexual wellness.

During our interview, she explained how difficult it was to get consumer insights in focus groups due to the very intimate nature of the category: *"It's hard to get the conversation about this taboo topic. So what we've done is create our own little community, people who are interested in talking about it. . . . It's so much about listening and creating [a space] for people to collaborate and have conversations."*

She noticed the powerful effect of somebody saying something that resonated with the group and everybody else in the group approving and building on it in a collaborative way: *"And then that's like a real insight for us to take that and bring that into our product development."*

COMBINES SMALL IDEAS INTO BIG ONES

We saw how ideas are fragile when they are small. A way to grow them is to combine them.

Great things are done by a series of small things brought together

VINCENT VAN GOGH[281]

This is especially true for disruptive innovation: *"The future of disruptive innovation is collaborative, it is actually implementing it and improvising on it day after day after day."*[282]

CREATES POWERFUL ECOSYSTEMS, INTERNAL AND EXTERNAL

I observed that the individuals from the "hot groups" started to be champions of collaboration in the company and were instrumental in building a company-wide culture of collaboration. It is a very interesting organic process. Collaboration is not built top-down by imposing it and "nominating" people to teams to improve collaboration. It's built bottom-up by people self-selecting and intentionally collaborating for their own growth and the benefit of the others and the organization.

It is true in big companies, and even more relevant for startups.

In our interview, Margaret Heffernan, author, mentor, and teacher, shared how: *"I would never have built the tech companies I built without astounding powerful creative technologists, engineers, designers; everything we did was a cross-disciplinary*

---

281 "Vincent Van Gogh Quotes," *Brainy Quote*, accessed September 24, 2020.

282 Ahmed Mohamed Maawy, "The future of disruptive innovation is collaborative," *Medium*, June 2, 2018.

collaboration. . . . I'm very grateful that they were willing to join a startup company in a way just to see what they could do and what they could do together."

The most powerful ecosystems are external.

Steve Johnson graphically describes how ideas grow thanks to collaboration and open innovation:

"A new idea is a new network of neurons firing in sync with each other inside your brain. And it turns out that, in fact, the network patterns of the outside world mimic a lot of the network patterns of the internal world of a human brain. We take ideas from other people, people we've learned from, people we run into in the coffee shop, and we stitch them together into new forms and we create something new. . . . The power—the marvelous, unplanned, emergent, unpredictable power—of open innovative systems. When you build them right, they will be led to completely new directions the creators never even dreamed of." [283]

This is what innovation truly is.

HELPS RETAIN TALENTS
True innovators are precious assets for the future of the enterprise.

---

283 *TED Talks,* "Steve Johnson: Where good ideas come from," TED Global 2010, video, 17:30.

Gusto reports that 37 percent of employees say "working with a great team" is their primary reason for staying.[284]

IS COLLABORATION FEMININE?

The short answer is: yes.

In her book *The Female Brain,* Louann Brizendine, MD, shows how due to their brain biology: *"Girls participate jointly in decision-making without display of status. Boys use language to command and get things done, brag, threaten, and ignore their partners' suggestions, and override each other's attempt to speak. Boys won't hesitate to take something they desire. Competition is part of their make up, they are more socially handicapped."*[285]

Margaret Heffernan describes a MIT study in one of her famous TED Talks, "Forget the pecking order at work."

The study shows that the really successful teams had three characteristics: *"First of all, they showed high degrees of social sensitivity to each other. Secondly, the successful groups gave roughly equal time to each other, so that no one voice dominated, but neither were there any passengers. And thirdly, the more successful groups had more women in*

---

284 Editorial team, "21 Collaboration Statistics that Show the Power of Team-work," *BIT.AI* (blog), September 2019.

285 Louann Brizendine, *The Female Brain* (New York: Broadway Books, 2006).

them. . . . What's key to that is their social connectedness to each other."[286]

Pat Roque, speaker, author, career transformation coach, and founder of the Rock On Success System, put those feminine skills to action in her career:

"Through collaboration, I realized that there were opportunities to connect dots that didn't exist. So how do you do that? You surround yourself with innovators, make sure that you are then able to elevate everyone's expert status. It's not about shining the light on me as a rock star alone. It's about making sure that all ships rise with the tide. So, my whole philosophy has always been about surrounding my people with geniuses. . . . It's not coming from a place of power. It's coming from a place of collective spirit, and collaboration and shared learning to really help make an impact in the world."

This is a very feminine trait grounded in humility. As we saw in Chapter 2, the masculine will want to play the solitary hero who saves the situation by fixing a problem. The feminine will not hesitate to ask for help and find the right competencies.

LET'S PRACTICE!

These are six of the best practices to develop collaboration for innovation. More resources, including workshops, are available on my website: www.innoveve.com.

---

286 *TED Talks*, "Margaret Heffernan: Forget the pecking order at work," TEDWomen 2015, video, 15:39.

☐ Share moments with the members of your group.
☐ Play.
☐ Practice with kids.
☐ Learn from biomimicry.
☐ Practice a team sport.
☐ Think "currencies" (value is not only money).

SHARE MOMENTS WITH THE MEMBERS OF YOUR GROUP
I already covered how having fun was important. You may think: this is because of your personality; you are joyful, but it may not apply to serious inventors.

Edison was not the single most important individual behind his inventions. Everything about his work was directly connected to other contributors. His success was dependent on their success in the lab.

"Edison also was known for the 'midnight lunch'—an endearing term coined by colleagues who would work on projects late into the night. According to author Sarah Miller Caldicott, Edison would leave the lab around 5 p.m. to have dinner with his family, but would return later to check in on the progress of his colleagues. It was then, surrounded by a close-knit group of trusted colleagues and the convivial atmosphere, that collaboration took its most pure and meaningful form in the Edison lab.

"At about 9 p.m., Edison would order in food for everyone from a local tavern. For an hour or so, the assembled crew would relax, tell stories, sing songs, and even play music together, before heading back to work until the wee hours of the morning.

They connected socially and created a deeper understanding of each other as people and not just workers. . . . For Edison, midnight lunch was crucially important. . . . creating an environment in which collaboration could thrive. It became a powerful link to Edison's use of small teams as a driver of innovation success."[287]

Do we need another proof that having fun is beneficial to innovation?

PLAY

For more than fifty years, most countries in the world have been gradually reducing children's opportunities to play. Decreasing playing leads to a big *"decline in the measure called 'creative elaboration,' which assesses the ability to take a particular idea and expand on it in an interesting and novel way."*[288]

Back in 2012, I met Luke Hohmann, who came for a meeting to introduce his company that was then called the Innovation Games Company. Its concept was to use games to create innovation, bringing teams together in a playful environment, up to the C-suite. They had developed very powerful games. I still remember them because to me that concept was right on.

---

287 Taylor Pipes, "Lessons in Collaboration & Creativity from Thomas Edison," *Medium*, May 18, 2017.

288 Peter Gray, "The play deficit," *Aeon*, accessed September 13, 2020.

PRACTICE WITH KIDS

As parents, it's important to prepare kids and show them the example by playing with them or having activities that require collaboration. Cooking, for instance, besides bringing gratitude, is a great exercise for collaboration: there are numerous tasks that can be managed by kids according to their abilities and preferences. The vision is clear, e.g. a yummy chocolate cake, and everyone can enjoy the result.

Kristen Thorson, a Getting Smart columnist, recommends tying the playful time to instruction and gives examples: *"Students learning about fractions might spend a weekend baking in the kitchen. Students learning about sorting might help organize toys or laundry. Students learning about trees might lead their family on a nature hike. By giving families ideas about how to connect home conversations and activities to the curriculum, students' instruction is enriched."*[289]

Kids learn how to collaborate at home; link it to work, so they collaborate at school, and it also helps parents practice collaboration.

LEARN FROM BIOMIMICRY

We already covered biomimicry in Chapter 7. Based on observation, it is more a discipline than a tool. There are many lessons we can take from nature about collaboration.

---

289 Kristen Thorson, "Creating a Culture of Collaborative Family Engagement," *Getting Smart,* April 20, 2018.

Let's come back to bees as an example. Bees are known to collaborate for group decisions to select a new hive or foraging through knowledge sharing. They are an inspiration for researchers at the University of Illinois at Urbana-Champaign, who are looking for ways to improve human collaboration during disaster relief efforts.

There are other great examples of collaboration in nature, like the mangrove forests. We can all get inspired by these models.[290]

PRACTICE A TEAM SPORT

In her book *Wolfpack,* Abby Wambach narrates how, as co-captain of Team USA and at thirty-five years old, she had to step off the field during the World Cup Championship in 2015. It was a tough decision. Abby could have "pouted," as she put it, because she could not lead her team to victory. Instead, she chose to "lead from the bench." I would say she was a great example of collaboration, bringing her unique skills and personality from wherever she was: leading on the field or cheering from the bench, it was still true collaboration with the common vision of winning together.

We won the world cup that year, we celebrated together, starters and bench players, as one team. I know in my bones that one of the reasons we won the 2015 World Cup was the support of the bench. The pride I feel about how I handled that tournament rivals the pride I had about scoring any big goal.

290 AskNature Team, "Honeybees collaborate when foraging, selecting a new hive through knowledge sharing," *Ask Nature,* August 18, 2016.

She talks a lot about the team in her book. She describes how a female team loves winning with joy, connectedness, and collaboration.[291]

Pat Roque summarized it in our interview:

The feminine traits for leadership apply to innovation: the humility to know that we are not supposed to be great at everything individually, but our collective team should be. So, the more that we can shine the light on the gifts and genius of others, the more that we can live and come from a place of gratitude. And the more we can collaborate and nurture with empathy.

THINK CURRENCIES

This great tool comes from my training with The Rhythm of Business.

When starting a collaboration, we need to have a balance between what we will bring and which benefits we will get.

When we think benefits, we usually think revenues.

The training helped us think differently about benefits in terms of "currencies," which are not limited to money. It depends on what you need the most in your current situation. A start-up at the beginning may need to partner to get funding, but a funded start-up may want to have access to expertise. A scientist with a patented technology may want

---

291 *Shona Project*, "Abby Wambach: Be the Wolf," July 5, 2018, video, 4:59.

access to manufacturing capabilities or a brand name. It's important to brainstorm and list the "currencies" for each collaboration partner.

'***'

We have reviewed the feminine innovation success formula and have seen how empathy, nurturing, inclusivity, intuition, and gratitude, when catalyzed by collaboration, lead to meaningful innovation that emotionally connects with consumers and creates value for the company: not only for the bottom line, but also by creating a better workplace and retaining talents. I shared successful examples from my professional career.

You may still wonder: how does this formula play in the bigger picture?

4

WHY DEVELOP YOUR FEMININE TRAITS?

15

THE FEMININE INNOVATION SUCCESS FORMULA WORKS

Let's dive into a story that illustrates the fact that the formula works in any industry and is not just a women's prerogative.

HOW A MAN INNOVATED
A MALE-DOMINATED INDUSTRY

Cyril Lignac was born in 1977 in Rodez, Aveyron, in Southwestern France. He grew up in a very loving environment that gave him strong values. He was not doing well at school, though, and his parents were wondering what they would do with him.

Today, Cyril Lignac is a renowned French chef. He is the owner of three restaurants: Le Chardenoux, Aux Prés et Le Bar des Prés; one cocktail bar: Dragon; five pastry shops: La Pâtisserie Cyril Lignac; and one chocolate shop: La

Chocolaterie Cyril Lignac. He will open the new restaurant Ischia in 2021. Chef Lignac is also a TV presenter for culinary programs on the French television channel M6 and signed a series of more than forty cookbooks that sold over three million copies.

HOW DID THAT HAPPEN?

He was still a kid when his grandmother gave him five hundred French francs for Christmas (this was quite a lot of money at that time). Cyril did something quite unexpected for a boy his age: he invited one of his friends to a Michelin three-star restaurant, the L'Auberge du Vieux Pont in Belcastel. The owner was a woman, Nicole Fagegaltier. Cyril loved the experience and had an epiphany: he decided cooking was his calling and he wanted to become a chef. He did something bold: he mustered the courage to call Nicole and tell her that he had lunch at her restaurant the day before and wanted to be her apprentice. As she answered that she never had an apprentice, he told her, "Well, this is your opportunity!"

What is fascinating about Cyril's career is that he didn't follow the usual path. The "haute cuisine" world is a very predominantly white male elitist world. It blatantly lacks diversity, which is especially true for women.[292] The percentage of women chefs with Michelin stars is only of 4.7 percent in the US and less than 3 percent in France.[293]

---

292 Laura Walkinshaw, "The Rise of the Female Michelin Star Chef," *Elite Traveler,* March 6, 2014.

293 Assia Labbas, "France's New Michelin Guide: More Fraternité Than Égalité," *The New York Times,* February 23, 2018.

Situations like this are better in other countries like the UK, but there is still a credibility issue. According to Sheila Dillon, presenter of BBC Radio 4's *The Food Programme*: *"Female chefs have brought in a new energy to professional kitchens, but investors don't seem as interested in investing in women as they do men."*[294]

"Women are doing such amazing stuff—yet we're still fighting to get recognized in the industry. It's still all about male chefs," says Romy Jill, the first female Indian head chef to open and run her own restaurant in the UK in 2013. She adds: "Running your own restaurant means long hours, and sexism and racism still exist whether we like to hear it or not."

Like in a lot of other industries, the #MeToo movement revealed lots of cases of sexual harassment in the kitchens, but violence is not limited to the sexual aspect. The cooking world is known for its bullying practices, with apprentices being forced to endure yelling, insults, slaps, and even punches—to the point that in 2014, several top chefs, including Cyril Lignac, gathered in Paris to denounce violence in French kitchens.[295]

It's a world that doesn't yet welcome people who are different, as Cyril Lignac quickly understood when he made his way to Paris in 2000 to work in the kitchen of L'Arpège, the restaurant of Chef Alain Passard.

---

294 Zara Morgan, "Why are our professional kitchens still male dominated?," *BBC News*, September 16, 2018.

295 Clea Caulcutt, "Paris chefs call for end to French kitchen violence," *BBC News*, November 9, 2014.

In an interview for the French magazine *l'OBS* in February 2020, Cyril explained how he had been mocked by the press for his look, his accent, and the fact that he married gastronomy and TV, which was considered vulgar. Famous chefs would just ignore him in official receptions.[296] Despite all these rebuffs, Cyril pursued his own path: his cooking is not driven by fame and making things beautiful and sophisticated; his objective is to make food accessible and make all his customers happy. As he wanted to reinvent his business, he closed his restaurant Le Quinzième after fifteen years. He lost the Michelin star in the process, but pursuing his passion was more important than fame.[297]

WOMEN ARE THE ONES—IRONICALLY IN THIS MASCULINE WORLD—WHO PAVED CYRIL'S CAREER

Cyril claims it himself:

Women are very important in my life because they have a delicacy, softness and pertinence that men don't have. . . . We need more women chefs![298]

The first woman was his mother. A children's nurse, she was very compassionate and protective. When he told her he wanted to be a chef she cried, not out of joy, not out of

---

296 "Cyril Lignac balances on the contempt of other chefs after his television debut," *PressFrom,* February 28, 2020.

297 Robert Brow, "Another Famous Parisian Chef Dumps on Michelin," *Michelin Scars,* June 14, 2019.

298 *Quotidien avec Yan Barthes,* "Invité: Cyril Lignac se raconte dans "Histoires de goûts"," March 6, 2020, video, 19:00.

sadness or anger, but just because she felt it was the right thing for him.

Cyril calls Nicole Fagegaltier his "mother in cooking." He recalls the distance he had with food when he was at the cooking school. He compares himself to a soccer player training just to become better. Nicole taught him to cook with more intimacy: he started to taste his dishes to make sure they would please his customers. Nicole rebalanced his cooking experience from performance toward pleasure. Cyril says that Nicole taught him everything about cooking: the rigor, the product, and permanent questioning.

In the early 2000s, Cyril Lignac was spotted by a woman, the producer Bibiane Godfroid, who bought the rights to the show Jamie's Kitchen by Jamie Oliver and broadcast it on French TV Channel 4. In a 2017 TV program, *Thé ou Café*, Bibiane recounted when she recommended Cyril for the *Oui Chef* show. At that time, chefs were stereotyped to be outspoken older men with a quite plump figure, not a young, timid, wiry character. Bibiane had been enthused by Cyril's genuine passion for food. Luckily, she could convince the network, as the show was a big success.[299]

Cyril continues to surround himself with women from the kitchen to the office, like his close collaborator Laurence Mentil.

---

299 *Theoucafe*, "Cyril Lignac—Intégrale du 14/10/2017—Thé ou Café," October 15, 2017, video, 39:53.

CYRIL'S COOKING HAS A FEMININE TWIST

IT'S DRIVEN BY EMOTIONS

First of all, his motivation and call to become a chef were not driven by ego and fame, but heart and passion. When the press asked him about his career plans, he just wanted to talk about cooking. Both his parents cooked at home, and one of his childhood memories is the benevolent attitude of the guests smiling while his parents performed this act of love: cooking for others. When reflecting on it today, Cyril recognizes that he just wanted to be loved. As he wouldn't be loved for his scholarship, he decided he would be loved as a chef.

I do things with my heart, with passion, and this takes a lot of energy.

Perigo Légasse, food and wine critic at the French magazine *Marianne*, summarized it beautifully when interviewed in the 2017 TV program *Thé ou Café*. He celebrated the fact that Cyril brings to the cooking profession not the sense of anxiety, pressure, threat, and humiliation present in a lot of cooking shows, but the sense of sharing, friendliness, happiness, pleasure, and indulgence.[300]

In other words, Cyril is shifting the profession from a masculine energy toward a feminine energy.

EMPATHY

By putting his customers and their pleasure first, his cooking is a model of *empathy*. It is very fashionable today for

---

300 *Theoucafe*, "Cyril Lignac—Intégrale du 14/10/2017—Thé ou Café," October 15, 2017, video, 39:53.

pastry chefs to create sophisticated desserts that are closer to art objects than food. It makes them look artistic, but what about their customers? Those desserts are out of reach for most of them.

Cyril understands that people want a pastry that tastes good, is affordable, and reminds them of their childhood, like the classical "chocolate éclair" cake or the infamous "marshmallow teddy bear" (I still have their taste in my mouth from my childhood days). He offers a wide range of recipes in his books, from very easy to complex, from appetizers to pastry. His motivation is that he wants to be relevant to anybody and make sure his customers are always happy.

INCLUSIVITY

Diversity is key in the kitchen. In his mixed-gender team, Cyril especially appreciates the serenity women bring to an environment that can easily turn chaotic. He creates a safe place of trust and collaboration that's also great for innovation, where they can learn and grow together, exchange, and debate. They practice *inclusivity* as each one brings their specific knowledge and expertise to the project.

NURTURING

Food is by definition an act of "nourishing." By not trying to impress his customers but pleasing them, Cyril nurtures their happiness and his relationship with them.

INTUITION

Cyril cooks from his heart and soul, following his *intuition*. As he is following his instinct, he is totally unable to say where he will be in fifteen years.

GRATITUDE

Cyril expresses a lot of *gratitude* for the people who supported him as we saw with his tribute to the women who were important in his life. He is also grateful for his life and to this profession that gave him everything.

COLLABORATION

Finally, in contrast to what's happening in most kitchens, where chefs are the absolute bosses, Cyril believes in *collaboration*. There are solid talents in his team who take their responsibilities. There is promotion and internal mobility; anyone can evolve inside the organization. The enterprise is growing and attracts talents.

An enterprise, it's a team. I love to be surrounded by collaborators full of desire and energy. This gives me a feeling of protection. I especially enjoy women as they bring a positive energy, not having this frantic search for power.[301]

Cyril may have made it to the top partly because he is a white male; however, he is imposing a style that is breaking with the conventional world of "haute cuisine." He is bringing empathy, nurturing, intuition, and collaboration to cooking for a more inclusive and diverse experience, hence opening the path for more women to bring their specific talents to the cooking world. He is proving that you can be successful by innovating from your heart and emotions.

---

301 *Theoucafe,* "Cyril Lignac—Intégrale du 14/10/2017—Thé ou Café," October 15, 2017, video, 39:53.

'***'

The formula can be applied to any industry.

Some feminine traits, like nurturing or intuition, are totally adapted to cooking, while empathy and collaboration may be more important in a technology industry. This is why the right dosage of the six "ingredients" (empathy, nurturing, inclusivity, intuition, gratitude, and collaboration) needs to be adapted to each innovation case.

$$Em + N + I_2G \overset{Co}{\dashrightarrow} \heartsuit + \$$$

'***'

We will now conclude, hoping that you have learned with each turn of a page and enjoyed the journey!

CONCLUSION

———

It was a gloomy afternoon in January 2020. I was sitting on my sofa, experiencing the down phase of the well-known entrepreneurial emotional roller coaster. I distractedly opened a LinkedIn message. It was from Tanya Alvarez, a young woman I had met in December at a neighbor's Christmas party who had expressed interest in my newly launched business. She was asking how the business was doing. As I answered honestly, she kindly offered to talk. After a while, she said: *"You need to write a book."*

Now you can just imagine me rolling my eyes and thinking *"Here we go again!"* Many of my friends had been telling me the same thing for years, and now also people I had just met.

Well, I am a talker; I am not a writer; I don't like to write; I am not skilled at it, not to mention in another language. Plus, I am a rebel, so the more somebody tells me to do something, the more I resist. . . . until the day *I* decide to do it.

Tanya found the way to change my mind, arguing that the book would be a wonderful way to showcase my experience.

"Huh?" I thought. I really wanted that but was not completely sold on the idea. This is when she revealed her "silver bullet": a twenty-week process that was based on research and community—she knew I was a scientist and loved to work with people, so she had pressed the right buttons. She connected me to Eric Koester, a professor from Georgetown who developed this "Book Creators" program. I was immediately seduced by Eric's passion and thought that I would learn so much and gather meaningful information in the process. The rest is history. This is how we are here today, and I really hope you enjoyed the journey as much as I did!

The title of this book could have been: "Innovation Has No Sex: Any Skill Welcome." As I researched about the masculine and the feminine, I realized that the future would be a non-gender one. This non-gendered view is still very aspirational though.

As a scientist, I looked at the facts: we still live in a (white) male-dominated world, so it may not be the right time to leapfrog.

Although I talked about men and women and had a gender discourse, the key message is that any human being can become a better innovator by rebalancing their innate traits between the masculine and feminine, wherever they stand on the gender spectrum. This is critical for innovation, as successful innovation requires using both masculine and feminine traits.

There is a blatant opportunity to act now, as we face a unique combination of:

- Business opportunity—the underserved $20+ trillion female market.
- Available talent pool with all the women innovators that have been kept out of the innovation table—and are naturally skilled at innovating.
- A need for the world to heal after all the recent crises by moving towards a more feminine energy of love and compassion.

I obviously tapped into my professional experience, but this book also reflects my personal journey from the masculine toward the feminine to become a more centered and happy human being.

I want to leave you with some fun homework.

I interviewed my friend Andrew Bennett, who I worked with when I was in the corporate world. Another fellow member of AMI (the innovation learning community you are now familiar with), Andrew is a keynote speaker, two-time TEDx presenter, leadership consultant, executive coach, and university professor.

I kept the best for the end: he is also a modern magician encouraging people to think about what they want to create in their lives using the three foundational acts of magic: why and what they want to create *(appear)*, what needs to go away *(disappear)*, and what needs to be healed *(restore)*.

Our discussion quickly turned into brainstorming (as always), and I thought: what a better way to end this book than by helping the readers take their learning and turn it into action, but in an entertaining way. Magic is about transformation and healing, which is a great objective for innovation.

You may want to take out a writing pad at this point, and I recommend you watch Andrew's TED Talk.[302] You may also go back to the practice lists at the end of Chapters 9 to 14.

Think about how you can reignite your innovation efforts. Don't hesitate to combine actions. They can be on the personal or the professional level. I provided some starter thoughts.

APPEAR: WHAT DO YOU WANT TO CREATE/INNOVATE?

You may want to:

- Start saying "No" to "pet" projects that don't go anywhere and consume your resources.
- Bring more diversity into your innovation team (especially young/old and different thinkers).
- Start walking meetings with your innovation partners (in nature when possible).
- Collaborate with your kids through activities like cooking or gardening.
- Create a thank-you ritual in your team.

---

302 TEDxSanJuanIsland, "Andrew Bennett: Practical Magic," June 2019, video, 19:03.

DISAPPEAR: WHAT DO YOU NEED TO LET GO OF TO BETTER INNOVATE?

You may want to let go of:

- Fear of failure.
- Meetings that don't move the innovation agenda.
- People in your team who don't have the right motivation (and find them a job where they will flourish).
- Consumer focus groups (where consumers tell you what you want to hear).
- Long hours on Netflix or social media (try picking up a book instead).

RESTORE: WHERE DO YOU NEED TO RECONNECT TO EMBRACE INNOVATION?

You may want to revive:

- Old relationships that brought you sadness (remember, it sparks empathy).
- Old projects/ideas that didn't work (maybe they were before their time and could be "healed").
- The feminine energy that resides in each of us (or the masculine one, depending on where you are in the gender spectrum).
- Your opinion on some colleagues who you may have judged too quickly.

'***'

It is your time to innovate your innovation.

Enjoy the magic and thank you!

ACKNOWLEDGEMENTS

———

I'd like to acknowledge those who are at the origin of this book: Tanya Alvarez, who connected me to the Book Creators program, and Eric Koester, whose passion for writing is contagious. Thanks for your guidance and generosity.

A big thank you to my publisher, New Degree Press, Brian Bies, my graphic designers Gjorgji Pejkovski and Liana Moisescu, and all my editors, especially Chelsea Olivia with whom I spent most of the time—intense working hours amidst laughter. You made this book a reality; thank you for pushing and motivating me.

If I may summarize my experience with all of you, it is: *"OMG! You were right about everything!"*

I'd also like to gratefully acknowledge my early readers: Alain Jacques, Albert Pettus, Alex Niel, Annette Raven, Anouke Steenvoort, Cheryl Perkins, Dan Trommater, David Kohistani, Joanie McCaw, Joe Ross, Kim Tutin, Marc Somnolet, Michelle Spehr, Peter Hilliard, Raul Maldonado, Rebecca Williams, Soren Kaplan, and Teresa Mendoza.

You did a fantastic job providing me with great comments and insights and definitely made a difference. It was worth your hard work! Most of you were also backers and/or cumulated with being interviewed; special thanks to those.

I had the privilege to interview wonderful people with diverse and fascinating backgrounds and experiences (some were also backers, thank you). I am grateful for the time you spent with me and all the insights that fed this book and the research behind it: Alexandra Fine, Alina Bilger, Amanda Pistocchi, Andrea Simon, Andrew Bennett, Anna Moine, Anne Hoag, Christy Curtis, Didier Roux, Doreen Steenland, Dr Kate Newburgh, Gregory Keyes, Ingrid Lindberg, John Downer, Judi Steward, Kaylie Dugan, Laurie Nicoll, Leslie Fleuranges, Lionel Yang, Lisa Lipkin, Maiko Kyogoku, Margaret Heffernan, Marilise de Villiers, Michelle Bottomley, Natalie Nixon, Nelida Quintero, Pat Roque, Peju O'Nile, Raj Sisodia, Razi Imam, Renee Riethmiller, Ron Carucci, Sophie Bailly-Maître, Yu Shi.

A big thank you to all the other people who backed my Indiegogo campaign. Big or small, your contribution went to my heart, and allowed me to be able to publish this book: Aima St Hunon, Alain Gendre, Alain and Nanou Duprat, Albert Elboudwarej, Aleksey Dumer, Amy Dresner-Yules, Andy Striso, Anita Nessin, Arleen Ashjian, Audra Morelock, Barbara Maimone, Cady North, Catherine Cluzeau, Caroline Rudd, Céline Marcelaud, Chelsea Patel, Chris Andrews, Christophe Mossé, Christopher Spires and Dustin Wilder, Chuck Wolfe, Claudia and Guillaume Piéchaud, Clémence Danko, Dana and Cody Harrison, Danielle Kaynor, Deborah Wright, Debra Lucenti, Dirk Devos, Domenico Trizio,

Dominique David, Elaine Broe, Elisa Devarieux, Elizabeth Misner, Ellen Julian, Emily Pan, France and Pascale Tronche, Francis Manaut, Frédéric and Valérie Crassat, Garance Aulagne, Gilles Brézélec, HanhLinh HoTran, Helmut Konz, Irina Sigalovsky, Jason L. Geno, Jean Doucet, Jean and Aline Devarieux, Jean-François and Christine Dupont, Jenny Heaton, Jenny Powers, Jeremie Gluckman-Picard, Joël and Chantal Bureau, Joëlle Bonnenfant, Karyn Zuidinga, Ken Coogan, Kim and Jo Fleming, Kristiina Hiukka, Laura Graziano, Laurent Simione, Lisa and Joe Robinson, Loïc, Myriam and Marion Jacquet, Lorenza Di Giovanni, Lucinda and Steven Salinas, Luke Hohmann, Mara Dumski, Margaret Rodgers, Marie-Claire Cailletaud and Jean-Pierre, Marija and George Heibel, Mary-Beth Robles, Mary-Chris Brauchli, Maryse and Joël Chardon, Matthieu Dejardins and Céline, Michael P. Robinson, Michael and Katherine Tesalona, Mohamed Omer, Myriam Peeters, Pat Clusman, Patrick Ferran, Philipp Lichtenberg, Philippe Joannis, René Bujard, Roland and Liliane Guenoun, Ron Growe, Sabrina Mucig and Laurent, Samantha Boulukos, Sharon, Bill and Morgan Burch, Shivani and Kashyap Bhatia, Somer Hackley, Stanislav Jaracz, Stephen Wiet, Steve Misner, Susan Diamond, Susan G Jackson, Sylvester Taylor, Tanya Laing, Thea Stauffenecker, Thomas Boyd, Tracy Gold, Uschi and Prudent Schröder, Wanda I Roman.

Contributions from such a diverse crowd (eleven countries!) comforted me in the fact that my message is quite universal.

I'd like to send a warm thank you to my family/friends (families Jacquet, Bureau, Devarieux). My friends are my extended family as mine is small. A special "wink" to my friends Caic and Cathy for forty+ years of friendship and for being with me in the ups and downs of life. Without forgetting my "211" neighbors who are so supportive in my daily life.

Lastly, I'd like to acknowledge the people (some I know, some I don't) who inspired me, during formal, informal, virtual, business, or fun events. All these conversations and exchanges were precious in informing the book and making it relevant.

All of you brought a piece to build the book I have the pleasure to launch today!

APPENDIX

___

INTRODUCTION

2020 Women on Board. "Accelerating Women into Corporate Boardrooms." Accessed August 22, 2020. https://2020wob.com/.

Bell, Alex, Raj Chetty, Xavier Jaravel, Neviana Petkova, and John Van Reenen. 2018. *Who Becomes an Inventor in America? The Importance of Exposure to Innovation, 2018,* from the Equality of Opportunity Project, team led by Stanford economist Raj Chetty. http://www.equality-of-opportunity.org/assets/documents/inventors_summary.pdf.

Budds, Diana. "The Female Engineers Building Better Sex Toys." *Fast Company,* March 31, 2017. https://www.fastcompany.com/90107296/the-female-engineers-building-better-sex-toys.

Contrera, Jessica. "The End Of 'Shrink It And Pink It': A History Of Advertisers Missing The Mark With Women." *The Washington Post.* June 9, 2016. https://www.huffpost.com/entry/

the-end-of-shrink-it-and-pink-it-a-history-of-advertisers-missing-the-mark-with-women_n_5759af4ce4b0ced23ca75725.

Fine, Alexandra. "Sex & Money." December 15, 2019. In *SPENT*. Produced by Lindsay Goldwert. Apple podcast, MP3 audio, 53:22. https://podcasts.apple.com/us/podcast/spent/id1104669965.

Glusac, Melina. "14 world-changing innovations by women that were originally credited to men." *Insider,* Mar 8, 2020. https://www.insider.com/inventions-by-women-credited-to-men-2018-9.

Green, Emma. "Innovation: The History of a Buzzword." *The Atlantic,* June 13, 2013. https://www.theatlantic.com/business/archive/2013/06/innovation-the-history-of-a-buzzword/277067/.

Gross,Rachel E. "The Clitoris, Uncovered: An Intimate History." *Scientific American,* March 4, 2020. https://www.scientificamerican.com/article/the-clitoris-uncovered-an-intimate-history/.

Hewlett, Sylvia Ann, Melinda Marshall, and Laura Sherbin. "How Women Drive Innovation and Growth." *Harvard Business Review,* August 23, 2013. https://hbr.org/2013/08/how-women-drive-innovation-and.

Hitti, Natashah. "CES restores Lora DiCarlo's sex toy award after sexism outcry." *Dezeen,* May 13, 2019. https://www.dezeen.com/2019/05/13/ces-restores-lora-dicarlos-sex-toy-award-after-sexism-outcries/.

Thompson, Derek. "The Secret to Smart Groups: It's Women." *The Atlantic*, January 18, 2015. https://www.theatlantic.com/business/archive/2015/01/the-secret-to-smart-groups-isnt-smart-people/384625/.

Shona Project. "Abby Wambach: Be the Wolf." July 5, 2018. Video, 4:59. https://www.youtube.com/watch?v=Fmvg-Myo8WM.

CHAPTER 1

DL, Vanida. "French Artist Restores Flea Market Paintings And Adds His Own Stories To Them." *Boredpanda*, posted 4 years ago, accessed August 23, 2020. https://www.boredpanda.com/restoring-modifying-classical-paintings-blase/?utm_source=-google&utm_medium=organic&utm_campaign=organic.

"Google: Innovation definition." Landing page. Accessed September 9, 2020. https://www.google.com/search?client=firefox-b-1-d&q=innovation+definition.

Hoque, Faisal. "10 Paradoxical Traits Of Creative People." *Fast Company*, September 4, 2013. https://www.fastcompany.com/3016689/10-paradoxical-traits-of-creative-people.

Idea to Value. "What is innovation? 15 innovation experts give us their definition." home page, accessed August 23, 2020. https://www.ideatovalue.com/inno/nickskillicorn/2016/03/innovation-15-experts-share-innovation-definition/.

Leveille, Ryan. "Hybrid Thinking" Leaders Will Prosper: Part 2—Humans Were Born to Create at Every Age." *Medium*, Feb 18, 2019. https://medium.com/crleveille/hybrid-thinking-leaders-will-prosper-part-2-humans-were-born-to-create-at-every-age-e616d6002fbe.

Online Etymology Dictionary, s.v."innovate," accessed August 23, 2020. https://www.etymonline.com/word/innovate.

Ringel, Michael, Ramón Baeza, Rahool Panandiker, Johann D. Harnoss. "Successful Innovators Walk the Talk—The Most Innovative Companies 2020." *BCG,* June 22, 2020. https://www.bcg.com/publications/2020/most-innovative-companies/successful-innovation.

Stanford News. "'You've got to find what you love,' Jobs says." *Stanford,* June 12, 2005. https://news.stanford.edu/2005/06/14/jobs-061505/.

CHAPTER 2

Beebe, Jeanette. "Fueling Gender." *Special Time Edition: the Science of Gender,* January 2020.

Dockterman, Eliana. "A doll For Everyone." *Special Time Edition: the Science of Gender,* January 2020.

eNCA, "Still defending the caveman." March 8, 2019. Video, 6:04. https://www.youtube.com/watch?v=ps65GwczWkA.

Encyclopoedia Universalis, 2nd ed. Paris: Encyclopædia Universalis SA., 1984.

Entis, Laura. "From Classroom To Work." *Special Time Edition: the Science of Gender,* January 2020.

Goldman, Bruce. "Two minds: The cognitive differences between men and women." *Stanford Medicine: Sex, gender and Medicine,* Spring 2017. https://stanmed.stanford.edu/2017spring/how-mens-and-womens-brains-are-different.html.

GRAZ. "Karissa Sanbonmatsu: What does it mean to be a woman?" January 19, 2020. Video, 25:56. https://www.youtube.com/watch?v=YdeChkf68eU.

Heid, Markham. "Biology and the Brain." *Special Time Edition: the Science of Gender,* January 2020.

Héritier, Francoise. *Masculin/féminin I: La pensée de la différence.* Paris: OJ.POCHE SC.HU., 2012. Kindle.

Ingalhalikar, Mdhura, Alex Smith, Drew Parker, Theodore D. Satterthwaite, Mark A. Elliott, Kosha Ruparel, Hakon Hakonarson, Raquel E. Gur, Ruben C. Gur, Ragini Verma. "Sex differences in the structural connectome of the human brain." PNAS January 14, 2014 111 (2) 823-828. https://doi.org/10.1073/pnas.1316909110.

Jantz, Gregory L.. "Brain Differences Between Genders." *Psychology Today,* February 27, 2014. https://www.psychologytoday.com/us/blog/hope-relationships/201402/brain-differences-between-genders.

Jana Kasperkevic. "Women Leaders: Stop Trying to Lead Like a Man: To be a true leader, you must establish trust and build bonds with your employees, says Simon Sinek." *Inc.,* May 8, 2013. https://www.inc.com/jana-kasperkevic/women-entrepreneurs-conference-simon-sinek.html.

Kret, M.E., B. de Gelder. "A review on sex differences in processing emotional signals." *Neuropsychologia* 50, no.7 (2012): 1211-1221. https://hdl.handle.net/11245/1.379478.

Macrae, Fiona. "Women talk more than men due to higher levels of Foxp 2 protein." *news.com.au,* February 21, 2013. https:// www.news.com.au/lifestyle/relationships/women-talk-more-than-men-due-to-higher-levels-of-foxp-2-protein/news-story/04572e67073ee0db7f0327847b0f53eb.

Pressfield, Stephen. "What is 'Female'?" *Writing Wednesdays* (blog). *Steven Pressfield,* August 21, 2019. https://stevenpressfield.com/2019/08/what-is-female/.

Wittman, Juliet. "Defending the Caveman explains the male of the species." *Westford,* September 26, 2013. https://www.westword.com/arts/defending-the-caveman-explains-the-male-of-the-species-5122078.

CHAPTER 3

2020 Women on Boards. "Accelerating Women into Corporate Boardrooms." Accessed August 22, 2020. https://2020wob.com/.

Adler, Laure, Camille Viéville. *"The Trouble with Women Artists: Reframing the History of Art."* Paris: Flammarion, 2019.

Berdahl, Jennifer L., Peter Glick, Marianne Cooper. "How Masculinity Contests Undermine Organizations, and What to Do About It." *Harvard Business Review,* November 02, 2018. https://

hbr.org/2018/11/how-masculinity-contests-undermine-organizations-and-what-to-do-about-it.

Catalyst. "*Women in Management: Quick Take.*" Accessed August 11, 2020. https://www.catalyst.org/research/women-in-management/.

Correll, Shelley J., Lori Mackenzie. "To Succeed in Tech, Women Need More Visibility." *Harvard Business Review,* September 13, 2016. https://hbr.org/2016/09/to-succeed-in-tech-women-need-more-visibility.

Fairchild, Caroline. "These male-dominated industries were hiring more women. Then COVID-19 happened." *LinkedIn News,* June 17, 2020. https://www.linkedin.com/pulse/male-dominated-industries-were-hiring-more-women-caroline-fairchild-1c/?trackingId=UqAR7Q6gQA66V5%2FsGu2H-FQ%3D%3D.

Google Arts &Culture. "The Women Painters Overlooked By Art History." Editorial Feature, Accessed August 22, 2020. https://artsandculture.google.com/theme/the-women-painters-overlooked-by-art-history/7AJCHFiEkqVKJg?hl=en.

Hodgson, Camilla. "Heels that turn into flats: the start-up taking the pain out of fashion." *Financial Times,* September 18, 2019. https://www.ft.com/content/07785d5c-d538-11e9-8367-807eb-d53ab77.

Melina Glusac. "14 world-changing innovations by women that were originally credited to men." *Insider,* March 8, 2020.

https://www.insider.com/inventions-by-women-credited-to-men-2018-9.

Green, Emma. "Innovation: The History of a Buzzword." *The Atlantic,* June 13, 2013. https://www.theatlantic.com/business/archive/2013/06/innovation-the-history-of-a-buzzword/277067/.

"Innovation vs Renovation." *Ask Difference,* Published August 13, 2020. https://www.askdifference.com/innovation-vs-renovation/.

Kanze, Dana, Laura Huang, Mark A. Conley, E. Tory Higgins. "Male and Female Entrepreneurs Get Asked Different Questions by VCs—and It Affects How Much Funding They Get." *HBR,* June 27, 2017. https://hbr.org/2017/06/male-and-female-entrepreneurs-get-asked-different-questions-by-vcs-and-it-affects-how-much-funding-they-get.

Lerchenmueller, Marc J., Olav Sorenson. "Research: Junior Female Scientists Aren't Getting the Credit They Deserve." *Harvard Business Review,* March 22, 2017. https://hbr.org/2017/03/research-junior-female-scientists-arent-getting-the-credit-they-deserve.

Lynkova, Darina. "Women in Technology Statistics: What's new in 2020?" *techjury.* June 22, 2020. https://techjury.net/blog/women-in-technology-statistics/#gref.

Meyers, Paul. "Managing and Communicating Innovation in a Startup." *Medium,* April 3, 2020. https://medium.com/

swlh/managing-and-communicating-innovation-in-a-start-up-b932b7a1a49.

Mohan, Pavithra. "These women entrepreneurs faced gender bias from their own employees." *Fast Company,* October 20, 2018. https://www.fastcompany.com/90241898/these-women-entrepreneurs-faced-gender-bias-from-their-own-employees.

Mohan, Pavithra. "This is what it's like to be the only female VC in the room." *Fast Company,* October 30, 2018. https://www.fastcompany.com/90253174/what-its-like-to-be-the-only-female-vc-at-a-firm.

Stembridge, Bob. "Women in Innovation: Gaining Ground, but Still Far Behind." *Scientific American.* May 3, 2018. https://blogs.scientificamerican.com/voices/women-in-innovation-gaining-ground-but-still-far-behind/.

Stanton, Alexandra. "10 ways women entrepreneurs can outwit "mansplaining" investors." Fast Company. November 5, 2018. https://www.fastcompany.com/90260442/10-ways-women-entrepreneurs-can-outwit-mansplaining-investors?utm_source=postup&utm_medium=email&utm_campaign=-FastCompanyDaily&position=2&partner=newsletter&campaign_date=11052018.

Tambini, Olivia. "10 female tech innovators you may not have heard of." *Techradar,* August 2018. https://www.techradar.com/news/10-female-tech-innovators-you-may-not-have-heard-of.

Watts, Ruth. *Women in Science: A Social and Cultural History.* London and New York: Rootledge, 2007.

Women In Innovation. "WIN's Founding Story." *WIN Women* (blog). *WIN's Founding Story,* January 9, 2019. https://womenininnovation.co/blog/wins-founding-story.

Wood, Johnny. "3 things to know about women in STEM11 Feb 2020." *World Economic Forum.* February 11, 2020. https://www.weforum.org/agenda/2020/02/stem-gender-inequality-researchers-bias/.

Wynn, Alison. "Why Tech's Approach to Fixing Its Gender Inequality Isn't Working." *Harvard Business Review.* October 11, 2019. UPDATED October 15, 2019. https://hbr.org/2019/10/why-techs-approach-to-fixing-its-gender-inequality-isnt-working.

CHAPTER 4

Brogaard, Berit. "Do Emotions Feel the Same Across Different Cultures?" *Psychology Today,* January 15, 2020. https://www.psychologytoday.com/us/blog/the-superhuman-mind/202001/do-emotions-feel-the-same-across-different-cultures.

Jerome, Richard. "Striving For The New." *Special Time Edition: the Science of Creativity,* August 2018.

Oppong, Thomas. "Psychologists Explain How Emotions, Not logic, Drive Human Behaviour." *Medium,* January 3, 2020. https://medium.com/personal-growth/psychologists-explain-how-emotions-not-logic-drive-human-behaviour-6ed0daf76e1a.

Penguin Random House. "Humans Are Underrated: What High Achievers Know That Brilliant Machines Never Will By Geoff Colvin." Accessed August 29, 2020. https://www.penguinrandomhouse.com/books/316067/humans-are-underrated-by-geoff-colvin/.

Popcorn, Faith, and Lys Marigold. *EVEOLUTION: Understanding women—8 essential truths that work in your business and your life.* New York: Hyperion, 2000.

Satell, Greg. "4 Ways Leaders Can Get More from Their Company's Innovation Efforts." *HBR,* October 10,2017. https://hbr.org/2017/10/4-ways-leaders-can-get-more-from-their-companys-innovation-efforts.

TED Talks. "Sandeep Jauhar: How your emotions change the shape of your heart." July 2019. Video, 15:54. https://www.ted.com/talks/sandeep_jauhar_how_your_emotions_change_the_shape_of_your_heart?utm_source=newsletter_daily&utm_campaign=daily&utm_medium=email&utm_content=image__2019-09-10.

TED Talks. "Simon Sinek: How freat leaders inspire action." September 2009. Video, 17:49. https://www.ted.com/talks/simon_sinek_how_great_leaders_inspire_action.

CHAPTER 5

Alammyan, Anangsha. "Will A Tampon Make Me Lose My Virginity?" *Medium,* May 27, 2020. https://medium.com/indelible-ink/tampons-and-virginity-a0900ff85e48.

Allied Market Research. "Report: Athleisure Market Out-look—2026." Accessed August 30, 2020. https://www.allied-marketresearch.com/athleisure-market.

Anderson-Jones, Rosa. "The Future of Beauty in 2018, with Anna Moine." *Timely,* January 7, 2018. https://www.gettimely.com/blog/beauty-in-2018-with-anna-moine/.

Barnish, Max, Heather May Morgan, Jean Barnish. "The 2016 High Heels: Health effects And psychosexual Benefits." *BMC Public Health* 18, 37 (2018). https://doi.org/10.1186/s12889-017-4573-4.

Bell, Diane. "Carmel high heel ban makes Ripley's." *The San Diego Union-Tribune,* September 10, 2014. https://www.sandiegouniontribune.com/sdut-carmel-eastwood-heels-ban-ordinance-ripley-book-2014sep10-story.html.

Contrera, Jessica. "The End Of 'Shrink It And Pink It': A History Of Advertisers Missing The Mark With Women." *The Washington Post,* June 9, 2016. https://www.huffpost.com/entry/the-end-of-shrink-it-and-pink-it-a-history-of-advertisers-missing-the-mark-with-women_n_5759af4ce4b0ced23ca75725.

Curves. Accessed August 30, 2020. https://www.curves.com/.

Dee, Harriet. "Why we don't want to give up our heels, even though they hurt." *Medium,* November 8, 2018. https://medium.com/@harriet_42632/why-we-dont-want-to-give-up-our-heels-even-though-they-hurt-5567307a0365.

Eliane Glaser. "Invisible Women by Caroline Criado Perez – a world designed for men." *The Guardian,* February 28, 2019.

https://www.theguardian.com/books/2019/feb/28/invisible-women-by-caroline-criado-perez-review.

Freedman, Paul, Chester D. Tripp. "How steak became manly and salads became feminine." *History News Network,* October 24, 2019. https://historynewsnetwork.org/article/173443.

Furness, Hannah. "Emily Blunt on Cannes heels row: 'everybody should wear flats'." *The Telegraph,* May 20, 2015. https://www.telegraph.co.uk/film/cannes-festival/emily-blunt-cannes-heel-row/.

Global Wellness Institute. "2018 Global Wellness Economy Monitor." Accessed August 30, 2020. https://globalwellnessinstitute.org/industry-research/2018-global-wellness-economy-monitor/.

Global Wellness Summit. "A New Feminist Wellness." 2018 Report. Accessed August 30, 2020. https://www.globalwellnesssummit.com/2018-global-wellness-trends/feminist-wellness/.

Griffin, Annaliese. "Women are flocking to wellness because modern medicine still doesn't take them seriously." *Quartz,* June 15, 2017. https://qz.com/1006387/women-are-flocking-to-wellness-because-traditional-medicine-still-doesnt-take-them-seriously/.

Hope Fashion. Accessed August 30, 2020. https://www.hopefashion.co.uk/us/.

Howland, Daphne. "For Nike, the future of sneaker innovation is female." *Retail Dive,* March 1, 2018. https://www.retaildive.

com/news/for-nike-the-future-of-sneaker-innovation-is-fe-
male/518162/.

Hung, Yie-Hsin. "51% of personal wealth in the US is controlled
by women." *WealthTrack*, June 28, .2019. https://wealthtrack.
com/51-percent-of-personal-wealth-in-the-u-s-is-controlled-
by-women/.

IHRSA Staff. "2018 Shows Continuing Uptrend of U.S. Health
Club Industry." *IHRSA*, April 12, 2019. https://www.ihrsa.org/
improve-your-club/industry-news/2018-shows-continuing-up-
trend-of-u-s-health-club-industry/.

Johnston, Chris. "Woman's high-heel petition receives 100,000-
plus signatures." *The Guardian*, May 12, 2016. https://www.
theguardian.com/world/2016/may/12/nicola-thorp-high-heel-
petition-receives-100000-plus-signatures.

Julian. "How Much Money Yoga With Adriene Makes On YouTube
– Net Worth." *Naibuzz*, last Updated on: April 14, 2020. https://
naibuzz.com/how-much-money-yoga-with-adriene-makes-
on-youtube-net-worth/.

Kanter, Rosabeth Moss. "For International Women's Day, Think
Outside the (Shoe)Box." *HBR*, March 7, 2011.https://hbr.
org/2011/03/for-international-womens-day-t.

Khazan, Olga. "Rise of the Lady Backpack." *The Atlantic*, May
3, 2019. https://www.theatlantic.com/health/archive/2019/05/
professional-women-are-wearing-backpacks/588619/.

Kremer, William. "Why did men stop wearing high heels?" *BBC News,* January 25, 2013. https://www.bbc.com/news/magazine-21151350.

Lines, Lisa M.. "The Myth of Female Hysteria and Health Disparities among Women." *RTI International,* May 9, 2018. https://www.rti.org/insights/myth-female-hysteria-and-health-disparities-among-women.

Merrill Lynch. "Women & Financial Wellness: Beyond the Bottom Line." Study in partnership with Age Wave, October 25–November 22, 2017. https://www.bofaml.com/content/dam/boamlimages/documents/articles/ID18_0244/ml_womens_study.pdf.

Morgan-Cole, Trudy. "Toxic Femininity." *Medium,* February 19, 2019. https://medium.com/@hypergraffiti/toxic-femininity-ecfe9fd9d8c5.

Morris, Paul, Jenny White, Edward Morrison, Kayleigh Fisher. "High Heels are Supernormal Stimuli: How Wearing High Heels Affects Judgments of Female Attractiveness." Evolution and Human Behavior 34, 3 (May 2013). https://hbr.org/2011/03/for-international-womens-day-t?autocomplete=true.

New Jersey Business. "Global Female Income to Reach $24 Trillion in 2020." *NJB Magazine,* March 6, 2020. https://njbmagazine.com/njb-news-now/global-female-income-to-reach-24-trillion-in-2020/.

Prasad, Ritu. "Eight ways the world is not designed for women." *BBC News,* June 5, 2019. https://www.bbc.com/news/world-us-canada-47725946.

Rafiq, Raifa. "I Believed That Tampons Were Impure." *Medium,* February 7, 2020. https://medium.com/refinery29/i-believed-that-tampons-were-impure-31b0f1901c97.

Segran, Elizabeth. "High Heels, Invented For The Male Gaze, Get A Feminist Makeover." *Fast Company,* April 13, 2018. https://www.fastcompany.com/40556015/meet-the-women-reinventing-the-high-heel-without-the-sexism.

Silverstein, Michael J., Kate Sayre. "The Female Economy." *HBR,* from the September 2009 Issue. https://hbr.org/2009/09/the-female-economy.

Sixth Tone. "Why Tampons Have Yet to Catch On in China." *Medium,* May 26, 2019. https://medium.com/@SixthTone/why-tampons-have-yet-to-catch-on-in-china-bca81873f0d4.

Universal Standard. Accessed August 30, 2020. https://www.universalstandard.com/.

World Footwear. "High heel sales fall as women shift to comfort." June 22, 2018. https://www.worldfootwear.com/news/high-heel-sales-fall-as-women-shift-to-comfort/3208.html

Yorke, Harry. "Employers can force women to wear high heels as Government rejects campaign to ban the practice." *The Telegraph,* April 21, 2017. https://www.telegraph.co.uk/

news/2017/04/21/government-rejects-ban-employers-forcing-women-wear-high-heels/.

CHAPTER 6

Ayres, Andrea. "Advice from my tampons." *Medium.* June 26, 2013. https://medium.com/@missafayres/advice-from-my-tampons-c8c7724de8cc.

Bellis, Mary. "A Brief History of the Tampon." *ThoughtCo,* updated June 21, 2019. https://www.thoughtco.com/history-of-the-tampon-4018968.

Bennett, Jessica and Mary Robinette Kowal. "Why NASA's First All-Women Spacewalk Made History." *The New York Times,* October 18, 2019. https://www.nytimes.com/2019/10/18/science/all-female-spacewalk-nasa.html.

Brooks Olsen, Hanna. "Centuries of Period Shame Kept Us from Getting THINX Sooner." *Medium,* July 12, 2017. https://medium.com/s/pulling-at-threads/centuries-of-period-shame-kept-us-from-getting-thinx-sooner-241ac880ec29.

Cartner-Morley, Jess. "Lean times and hemlines." *The Guardian,* October 31, 2008. https://www.theguardian.com/lifeandstyle/2008/nov/01/financial-crisis-fashion.

Causeartist. "Conscious Period Created Social Impact Tampons To Provide A Healthier Option To All Women." *Medium,* July 27, 2016. https://medium.com/@Causeartist/conscious-period-created-social-impact-tampons-to-provide-a-healthier-option-to-all-women-889a1df89118.

Cherian, Anna E.. "My Experience Converting From Pills, Tampons, & Calendars to Paragard IUD, THINX, Diva Cup, & Clue." *Medium,* July 10, 2017. https://medium.com/@annacherian/my-experience-converting-from-pills-tampons-calendars-to-paragard-iud-thinx-diva-cup-clue-83ff22abbf4c.

Christensen, Christian. "We Can Learn a Lot from Dancing Swedish Tampons." *Medium,* October 21, 2015. https://medium.com/@ChrChristensen/we-can-learn-a-lot-from-dancing-swedish-tampons-7dfod92417a2.

Dee, Harriet. "Why we don't want to give up our heels, even though they hurt." *Medium,* November 8, 2018. https://medium.com/@harriet_42632/why-we-dont-want-to-give-up-our-heels-even-though-they-hurt-5567307a0365.

Elmhirst, Sophie. "Tampon wars: the battle to overthrow the Tampax empire." *The Guardian.* February 11, 2020. https://www.theguardian.com/society/2020/feb/11/tampon-wars-the-battle-to-overthrow-the-tampax-empire?utm_source=pocket&utm_medium=email&utm_campaign=pockethits.

Frigelis, Yana. "What It's Like to Tour Jaipur With One of India's First Female Rickshaw Drivers." *AFAR,* Apr 9, 2018. https://www.afar.com/magazine/what-its-like-to-take-a-tour-with-the-ladies-of-the-pink-city?.

Funding Universe. "Johnson & Johnson History." Accessed September 6, 2020. http://www.fundinguniverse.com/company-histories/johnson-johnson-history/.

Girls Who Code. "Andrea Gonzales: Throwing Tampons at Gender Biases." February 21, 2016. https://medium.com/@GirlsWho-Code/andrea-gonzales-throwing-tampons-at-gender-biases-4a165d7845d8.

Kaplan, Soren. "Mothers Of Invention: How Moms Help Huggies Innovate." *Fast Company,* August 6, 2012. https://www.fastcompany.com/3000151/mothers-invention-how-moms-help-huggies-innovate.

Kay, Karen. "Digging their heels in: women wage war on footwear dress codes." *The Guardian,* June 8, 2019. https://www.theguardian.com/fashion/2019/jun/08/why-women-in-japan-are-fighting-high-heel-dress-codes-at-work-global-support.

Landon Funk. "Sick Of Wasting Your Money On Tampons? Try LunaPads Like We Did." *Funky Feminist* (blog), accessed September 8, 2020. https://www.funkyfeminist.com/blog/lunapads.

Long, Liz. "Why Products Designed By Women Are The Next Big Thing." *Forbes,* December 22, 2017. https://www.forbes.com/sites/lizlong/2017/12/22/why-products-designed-by-women-are-the-next-big-thing/amp/.

New Jersey Business. "Global Female Income to Reach $24 Trillion in 2020." *NJB Magazine,* March 6, 2020. https://njbmagazine.com/njb-news-now/global-female-income-to-reach-24-trillion-in-2020/.

The Museum of Menstruation and Women's Health. "Inside Mum 6." Accessed September 6, 2020. http://www.mum.org/CuradsKotexads.htm.

w.in.. "The Path Forward for Female Founders." June 16, 2020. Video, 33:48. https://www.youtube.com/watch?v=Dg5sJoyPt-jk&feature=youtu.be.

Wei-Haas, Maya. "First all-woman space walk puts spotlight on spacesuit design." *National Geographic,* October 18, 2020. https://www.nationalgeographic.com/science/2019/10/first-all-women-spacewalk-suit-design/.

CHAPTER 7

AZ QUOTES. "Janine Benyus Quotes." Accessed October 12, 2020. https://www.azquotes.com/author/22304-Janine_Benyus.

Babson College. "More Than 250M Women Worldwide Are Entrepreneurs, According to the Global Entrepreneurship Monitor Women's Report from Babson College and Smith College." *PR Newswire,* November 18, 2019. https://www.prnewswire.com/news-releases/more-than-250m-women-worldwide-are-entrepreneurs-according-to-the-global-entrepreneurship-monitor-womens-report-from-babson-college-and-smith-college-300960196.html.

Baynes, Chris. "Women entrepreneurs less likely to quit their business than men, say researchers." *Independent,* September 4, 2019. https://www.independent.co.uk/news/business/news/women-business-entrepreneurs-quit-men-study-liverpool-university-a9090306.html.

Cybersecurity Ventures. "Women Know Cyber." Accessed September 7, 2020. https://cybersecurityventures.com/wp-content/uploads/2019/05/Women_Know_Cyber.pdf.

Frost & Sullivan. "Cybersecurity in the Power Industry." July 10, 2017. Accessed September 7, 2020. https://ww2.frost.com/frost-perspectives/cybersecurity-in-the-power-industry/.

Fundera. "17 Women-Owned Business Stats You Need to Know." *Fundera,* accessed September 6, 2020. https://www.fundera.com/resources/women-owned-business-statistics.

Global Wellness Institute. "RESETTING THE WORLD WITH WELLNESS: Food as Nourishment for Body, Mind, and Spirit." *Global Wellness Institute,* June 3, 2020. https://globalwellnessinstitute.org/wp-content/uploads/2020/06/Resetting-the-World-with-Wellness-Food-as-Nourishment3.pdf.

Hewlett, Sylvia Ann, Melinda Marshall, and Laura Sherbin. "How Women Drive Innovation and Growth." *Harvard Business Review,* August 23, 2013. https://hbr.org/2013/08/how-women-drive-innovation-and.

Jaggard, Victoria. "Why science matters in a tough time." *National Geographic,* June 3, 2020. https://www.nationalgeographic.com/newsletters/science/2020/06/why-science-matters-tough-time-june-03/.

Jaramillo, Estrella. "Women Investing In Femtech II: Closing the Gender Gaps in Investment and Health Innovation." *Forbes,* August 26, 2019. https://www.forbes.com/sites/estrellajaramillo/2019/08/26/women-investing-in-femtech-ii-closing-the-gender-gaps-in-investment-and-health-inno-vation/#6635830a657a.

Keb' Mo'. "Keb' Mo'—Put a Woman in Charge feat. Rosanne Cash (Official Music Video)." October 11, 2018. Video. 4:04. https://www.youtube.com/watch?v=FciQeRGYFlw&feature=youtu.be.

Lindzon, Jared. "Female entrepreneurs are just as resilient as men–despite lower revenue." *Fast Company,* March 1, 2019. https://www.fastcompany.com/90307659/female-entrepreneurs-are-just-as-resilient-as-men-despite-lower-revenue.

Livesey, Rebecca. "Feminine Energy Holds the Key to the Future of Entrepreneur Leadership." *Entrepreneur,* March 8, 2019. https://www.entrepreneur.com/article/329871.

McFall-Johnsen, Morgan. "The fashion industry emits more carbon than international flights and maritime shipping combined. Here are the biggest ways it impacts the planet." *Business Insider,* October 21, 2019. https://www.businessinsider.com/fast-fashion-environmental-impact-pollution-emissions-waste-water-2019-10.

Medal, Andrew. "4 Cyber Security Risks Your Employees Must Know (and How They Can Be Prepared)." *Inc.,* October 2, 2017. https://www.inc.com/andrew-medal/4-cyber-security-risks-your-employees-must-know-about-how-to-prepare-for-them.html.

Merrill Lynch. "Women & Financial Wellness: Beyond the Bottom Line." Study in partnership with Age Wave, October 25–November 22, 2017. https://www.bofaml.com/content/dam/

boamlimages/documents/articles/ID18_0244/ml_womens_
study.pdf.

Satell, Greg. "Why We Need Women to Have a Larger Role in
Innovation." *Inc.*, November 17, 2018. https://www.inc.com/
greg-satell/why-we-need-women-to-have-a-larger-role-in-in-
novation.html.vi.

Smith, Sonia. "Unfriendly Climate." *Pocket*, accessed September 6, 2020, originally appeared on Texas Monthly and was
published April 15, 2016. https://getpocket.com/explore/item/
unfriendly-climate.

TED. Talks "Katharine Wilkinson: How empowering women and
girls could stop global warming." TED Women 2018. Video.
13:40. https://www.ted.com/talks/katharine_wilkinson_how_
empowering_women_and_girls_can_help_stop_global_
warming/transcript?language=en.

TED Talks. "Ivonne Roman: How policewomen
make communities safer." TED 2019. Video. 5:44.
https://www.ted.com/talks/ivonne_roman_how_police-
women_make_communities_safer#t-337402.

TEDx Talks. "Innovation Powered by Women | MacKenzie Roe-
buck-Walsh | TEDxRapidCity." July 10, 2015. Video, 6:46.
https://www.youtube.com/watch?v=RogUOtdjTAM.

w.in.. "Discussion with Dr Miriam Merad: Getting more women
in STEM." June 16, 2020. Video, 36:08. https://www.youtube.
com/watch?v=fkcADMiPwSY&feature=youtu.be.

w.in.. "Together for the planet, right here, right now." June 16, 2020. Video, 42:23. https://www.youtube.com/watch?v=XRc-oDhR-mUY&feature=youtu.be.

CHAPTER 8

13h15 le dimanche. "Abeilles to bee or not to be." January 18. 2018. Video, 45:58. https://www.youtube.com/watch?v=2tyUOoR-zGso.

Bhat, Nilima, Raj Sisodia. *Shakti Leadeship: Embracing Feminine and Masculine Power in Business.* Oakland: Berrett-Koehler, 2016.

Freeman, Jacqueline. *Song of Increase: Listening to the Wisdom of Honeybees for Kinder Beekeeping and a Better World.* Boulder: Sounds True, 2016.

CHAPTER 9

Brizendine, Louann. *The Female Brain.* New York: Broadway Books, 2006.

Cosgrove, Julia. "What Travel Can Teach Us About Empathy." *AFAR,* Feb 14, 2020, from the March/April 2020 issue. https://www.afar.com/magazine/what-travel-can-teach-us-about-empathy?.

Dettman, Caroline, Erin Gallagher and Pamela Culpepper. "Forget returning to work as 'normal'—this is what should take its place." *Fast Company,* April 29, 2020. https://www.fastcompany.com/90498045/forget-returning-to-work-as-normal-this-is-what-should-take-its-place?.

Donnelly, Caroline. "Microsoft CEO Satya Nadella on why empathy is essential for technology innovation." *Computer-Weekly,* October 2, 2017. https://www.computerweekly.com/news/450427356/Microsoft-CEO-Satya-Nadella-on-why-empathy-is-an-essential-for-technology-innovation.

Gallagher, Brian. "Taking Another Person's Perspective Doesn't Help You Understand Them." *Facts So Romantic* (blog), *Nautilus.* June 27, 2018. http://nautil.us/blog/taking-another-persons-perspective-doesnt-help-you-understand-them.

Pedersen, Traci. "Reading Fiction May Boost Empathy." *PsychCentral,* August 8, 2018. https://psychcentral.com/news/2016/07/20/reading-fiction-boosts-empathy/107399.html.

REDEF. "Charles Chu: The Polymath Project: The ABCs of Fake Empathy."Accessed September 8, 2020. https://redef.com/author/58b9e2a2f6843425b3b10433.

Stern Robin, Diane Divecha. "The Empathy Trap." *Psychology Today,* published May 4, 2015, last reviewed on June 15, 2016. https://www.psychologytoday.com/us/articles/201505/the-empathy-trap.

Weiss, John P.. "This Is The Unexpected Power of Sadness." *Medium,* December 18, 2018. https://medium.com/personal-growth/this-is-the-unexpected-power-of-sadness-4f296618c30d.

Working a Better Life. "Probably T.he Most Valuable Business Skill You Can Learn." August 9, 2019. https://workingaobetterlife. com/probably-the-most-valuable-business-skill-you-can-learn/.

CHAPTER 10

Andreasen, Nancy C.. "Secrets of the Creative Brain." *The Atlantic,* July/August 2014 Issue. https://www.theatlantic.com/magazine/archive/2014/07/secrets-of-the-creative-brain/372299/.

Biglan, Anthony, Brian R. Flay, Dennis D. Embry, Irwin N. Sandler. "The Critical Role of Nurturing Environments for Promoting Human Wellbeing." *Am Psychol.* 2012 May-Jun; 67(4): 257–271, doi: 10.1037/a0026796. https://www.ncbi.nlm.nih.gov/pmc/articles/PMC3621015/.

Brizendine, Louann. *The Female Brain.* New York: Broadway Books, 2006.

CBInsights. "Foot In Mouth: 59 Quotes From Big Corporate Execs Who Laughed Off Disruption When It Hit." November 12, 2019. https://www.cbinsights.com/research/big-company-ceos-execs-disruption-quotes/.

Chopra, Mallika. "A Meditation on Nurturing and Giving." *SONIMA,* accessed September 10, 2020. https://www.sonima.com/meditation/meditation-on-nurturing/.

Cohen, Steven. "How Meditation Strengthens the 4 Pillars of Leadership." *Mindful Leaders* (blog), October 15, 2019. https://www.

mindfulleader.org/blog/32085-how-meditation-strengthens-the-4-pillars?.

Dal Porto, Christopher. "Innovation Requires Nurturing." *Medium,* March 29, 2017. https://medium.com/@csdalporto/innovation-requires-nurturing-21e09fb7ad8e.

Dictionary Online, s.v. "*incubator*". Accessed September 10, 2020. https://www.dictionary.com/browse/incubator.

Global Wellness Summit. "Successful Brands of the Future Will Be "Nature Smart"." Trendium, accessed September 10, 2020. https://www.globalwellnesssummit.com/trendium/successful-brands-of-the-furture-will-be-nature-smart/.

Gaynes, Robert. "The Discovery of Penicillin—New Insights After More Than 75 Years of Clinical Use." *Emerg Infect Dis.,* 2017 May; 23(5): 849–853, doi: 10.3201/eid2305.161556. https://www.ncbi.nlm.nih.gov/pmc/articles/PMC5403050/.

Irving, Michael. "Eight of the worst ideas to ever cross Kickstarter." *New Atlas,* January 05, 2019. https://newatlas.com/worst-kickstarter-campaigns/57827/.

"Jean Cocteau Quotes." *Good Reads.* Accessed October 7, 2020. https://www.goodreads.com/author/quotes/23993.Jean_Cocteau.

LegoTEG Creations. "Remote Controlled Suitcase." March 24, 2018. Video. 4:21. https://www.youtube.com/watch?v=zwIcZlCZA4s.

Milenkovic, Jovan. "How Many iPhones Have Been Sold World-wide? – iPhone Sales Analyzed." *Kommando Tech,* February 11, 2020. https://kommandotech.com/statistics/how-many-ip-hones-have-been-sold-worldwide/.

Murray, Lisa. "Nurturing Business Brilliance." *Medium,* Octo-ber28, 2015. https://medium.com/@lisamurray/nurturing-busi-ness-brilliance-54ba1c774dce.

"Nurture Quotes." *Good Reads.* Accessed September 23, 2020. https://www.goodreads.com/quotes/tag/nurture.

Sacks, Oliver. "The healing power of gardens." *The New York Times,* April 18, 2019. https://www.nytimes.com/2019/04/18/opinion/sunday/oliver-sacks-gardens.html.

Shenton, Renee. "Q&A with Dr. Thomas J. Fogarty: How the Fog-arty Institute for Innovation is nurturing breakthroughs in medical technology." *Medium,* December 24, 2014. https://medium.com/breakout-labs/q-a-with-dr-thomas-j-fogarty-how-the-fogarty-institute-for-innovation-is-nurturing-break-throughs-in-643187633fec.

Sizelove, Valerie. "What Gardening Teaches You About Love." *Medium,* June 25, 2018. https://medium.com/@herfreelance/what-gardening-teaches-you-about-love-5e92b8705928.

Special Time Edition: the Science of Creativity, "Chapter One: The Creative Animal." August 2018.

Tank, Aytekin. "Get outside: how nature can boost your health & creativity."*Jotform*. March 5, 2020. https://www.jotform.com/blog/power-of-nature/.

Tapia, Ash. "Nurturing Innovation Is F*****g Hard." *Medium,* November 11, 2017. https://medium.com/@asfaq/nurturing-innovation-is-f-g-hard-ca7823e07b0c.

Satell, Greg. "Innovation Isn't About Ideas." *Medium,* October 6, 2018. https://medium.com/s/story/4-things-nobody-ever-tells-you-about-innovation-5a9168b89968.

Sister. "Jennifer Armburst: Proposals for the Feminine Economy." Accessed September 10, 2020. https://sister.is/proposals-for-the-feminine-economy.

smugmacgeek. "Ballmer Laughs at iPhone." September 18, 2007. Video, 2:22. https://www.youtube.com/watch?v=eywioh_Y5_U.

TED Talks. "Steve Johnson: Where good ideas come from." TED Global 2010. Video, 17:30. https://www.ted.com/talks/steven_johnson_where_good_ideas_come_from?language=en.

CHAPTER 11

AFP. "Hip cafe chain staffed by workers with Down syndrome opens in Paris." *The Local,* March 23, 2018. https://www.thelocal.fr/20180323/hip-cafe-chain-staffed-by-down-syndrome-staff-opens-in-paris.

Austin, Robert D., Gary P. Pisano. "Neurodiversity as a Competitive Advantage." *HBR,* from the May–June 2017 Issue. https://hbr.org/2017/05/neurodiversity-as-a-competitive-advantage.

Bourke, Juliette, Bernadette Dillon. "The diversity and inclusion revolution: Eight powerful truths." *Deloitte Insights.* Deloitte Review, issue 22. Accessed September 24, 2020. https://www2.deloitte.com/us/en/insights/deloitte-review/issue-22/diversity-and-inclusion-at-work-eight-powerful-truths.html.

Cho, Janet H.. ""Diversity is being invited to the party; inclusion is being asked to dance." Verna Myers tells Cleveland Bar." *Cleveland,* updated January 11, 2019; posted May 25, 2016. https://www.cleveland.com/business/2016/05/diversity_is_being_invited_to.html.

"COLGATE BRIGHT SMILES, BRIGHT FUTURES®". *Colgate-Palmolive.* Accessed September 13, 2020. https://www.colgate.com/en-us/bright-smiles-bright-futures.

Foley, Katherine Ellen. "How the human brain stays young even as we age." *Quartz,* November 19, 2019. https://qz.com/1708872/the-human-brain-is-the-most-resilient-organ-in-the-body/?.

Haimerl, Amy. "The fastest-growing group of entrepreneurs in America." *Fortune,* June 29, 2015. https://fortune.com/2015/06/29/black-women-entrepreneurs/.

Johnson, Don. "How 'Verbal Aikido' Can Help You Avoid Stupid Arguments." *Human Parts,* September 7, 2020. https://humanparts.medium.com/why-its-easy-to-get-into-stupid-arguments-8c6f2310685b.

Kagumire, Rosebell. "The cost of diversity without inclusion." *Reflection and Rumination* (blog). *How Matters.* June 8, 2018. http://www.how-matters.org/2018/06/08/the-cost-of-diversity-without-inclusion/.

Martin, Courtney. "When Diversity Is Just About "Optics". It Doesn't Count." *Medium,* July 26, 2018. https://brightthemag.com/diversity-good-optics-doesnt-count-white-progressives-race-sex-inclusion-a4264b89288.

Mitchnick, Mark. "Our Two Brains, Mindfulness, and Decision-Making." *Mindful Leader,* July 1, 2019. https://www.mindfulleader.org/blog/27302-our-two-brains-mindfulness-and-decision.

NBC News. "Anand Giridharadas." Accessed September 7, 2020. http://www.nbcnews.com/ID/41297019.

NPR News staff. "The Grown-Up Brain': Sharper Than Once Thought." *NPR News,* April 20, 2010. https://www.npr.org/templates/story/story.php?storyId=126115275.

Obama, Michelle. *Becoming.* Barnes & Noble. Retrieved November 18, 2018. https://www.barnesandnoble.com/w/becoming-michelle-obama/1128038172.

Phillips, Michelle, John Cigno. "Promoting Diversity, Practicing Inclusion, and Driving Positive Change in the Legal Industry." *INSIGHT Into Diversity,* July 2, 2018. https://www.insightintodiversity.com/promoting-diversity-practicing-inclusion-and-driving-positive-change-in-the-legal-industry/.

Radd, Vanessa. "International Women's Day: Celebrating diversity and inclusiveness in Aikido #AikidoWomen." *Medium,* March 7, 2018. https://medium.com/@vanradd/international-womens-day-celebrating-diversity-and-inclusiveness-in-aikido-aikidowomen-9cc10fe40ba4.

TED Talks. "Poet Ali: The language of being human." TEDSummit 2019. Video, 14:47. https://www.ted.com/talks/poet_ali_the_language_of_being_human?.

Tigar, Lindsay. "How these 3 women entrepreneurs launched their businesses after 40." *Fast Company,* February 28, 2019. https://www.fastcompany.com/90309220/how-these-3-women-entrepreneurs-launched-their-businesses-after-40?.

"The meaning and origin of the expression: Necessity is the mother of invention." *The Phrase Finder,* accessed September 24, 2020. https://www.phrases.org.uk/meanings/necessity-is-the-mother-of-invention.html.

Zarya, Valentina. "The fastest-growing group of entrepreneurs in the U.S.? Minority women." *Fortune,* August 21, 2015. https://fortune.com/2015/08/21/women-small-business-diverse/.

CHAPTER 12

Birsel, Ayse. *Design the Life you Love: a step-by-step guide to building a meaningful future.* Berkeley: Ten Speed Press, 2015.

Boston College. "Trust your gut: Intuitive decision-making based on expertise may deliver better results than analytical approach." *Science Daily,* December 20, 2012. https://www.sciencedaily.com/releases/2012/12/121220144155.htm.

Dean, Nicole. "Stepping Up Your Creativity: Walking, Meditation, and the Creative Brain." *Brain World,* August 21, 2020. https://brainworldmagazine.com/stepping-creativity-walking-meditation-creative-brain/.

Denning, Tim. "Choose Minimalism to Make Life Easier on Yourself." *Medium,* December 27, 2019. https://medium.com/@timdenning/choose-minimalism-to-make-life-easier-on-yourself-a045a6fae72c.

Green, Penelope. "Sleep Is the New Status Symbol." *The New York Time,* April 8, 2017. https://www.nytimes.com/2017/04/08/fashion/sleep-tips-and-tools.html.

Gross, Daniel A.. "This Is Your Brain on Silence: Contrary to popular belief, peace and quiet is all about the noise in your head." *Nautilus,* July 7, 2016. http://nautil.us/issue/38/noise/this-is-your-brain-on-silence-rp.

Hutson, Matthew. "Selfishness Is Learned: We tend to be cooperative—unless we think too much." *Nautilus,* June 9, 2016. http://nautil.us/issue/37/currents/selfishness-is-learned.

Kasanoff, Bruce. "Intuition Is The Highest Form Of Intelligence." *Forbes,* February 21, 2017. https://www.forbes.com/sites/brucekasanoff/2017/02/21/intuition-is-the-highest-form-of-intelligence/#38329eb43860.

Lee, Janice. "What Humanity Can Learn From Plants: On trees, moss, and feeling at a distance." *Medium,* May 24, 2018. https://medium.com/s/off-beat/what-humanity-can-learn-from-plants-efece7acd3ao.

Liu, Gloria. "Walking Is Making a Major Comeback." *Outside,* June 8, 2020. https://www.outsideonline.com/2414207/walking-popularity-comeback-coronavirus?utm_source=pocket-newtab#close.

Mahoney, Sarah. "How Intuitive Are You? Take This Quiz To Find Out—And See How To Sharpen Your 6th Sense." *Prevention,* September 2, 2015. https://www.prevention.com/life/a20477104/gut-feelings-and-intuition/.

Maldarelli, Claire. "How many hours of sleep do you actually need? It depends on how well you want your brain to work." *Popular Science,* April 11, 2017. https://www.popsci.com/how-many-hours-sleep-do-you-actually-need/.

Mecking, Olga. "The Case for Doing Nothing: Stop being so busy, and just do nothing. Trust us." *The New York Times,* April 29, 2019. https://www.nytimes.com/2019/04/29/smarter-living/the-case-for-doing-nothing.html.

Mishler, Adriene. "Hello Fear." *Yoga with Adriene* (blog), accessed October 8, 2020. https://yogawithadriene.com/hello-fear/.

Misirlisoy, Erman. "Why You Write Better When You Travel." *Medium,* March 9, 2020. https://medium.com/@ermanmisirlisoy/why-you-write-better-when-you-travel-197d9b2f08e5.

Nierenberg, Cari. "The Science of Intuition: How to Measure 'Hunches' and 'Gut Feelings'." *Live Science*, May 20, 2016. https://www.livescience.com/54825-scientists-measure-intuition.html.

Oakley, Colleen. "The Power of Female Intuition." *WebMD*, August 12, 2012. https://www.webmd.com/balance/features/power-of-female-intuition#1.

Perez, Carlos E.. "The Link Between Sleep and Deep Learning." *Medium*, May 31, 2018. https://medium.com/intuitionmachine/the-link-between-sleep-and-deep-learning-5f7d347cc789.

Riggio, Ronald E. "Women's Intuition: Myth or Reality? It's mostly reality." *Psychology Today*, July 14, 2011. https://www.psychologytoday.com/us/blog/cutting-edge-leadership/201107/women-s-intuition-myth-or-reality.

Schwartz, Tony. "Relax! You'll Be More Productive." *The New York Times*, February 9, 2013. https://www.nytimes.com/2013/02/10/opinion/sunday/relax-youll-be-more-productive.html?campaign_id=33&instance_id=12063&segment_id=16658&user_id=74d89d7f65f676bade014494bcf0e981&regi_id=93209750.

Series: Success with Moira Forbe. "Silicon Valley Power Player Kirsten Green On Getting Ahead With Gut Instinct." Forbes. October 24, 201. Video, 5:11. https://www.forbes.com/video/6097122163001/#1c0e2d586d07.

Tank, Aytekin. "Entrepreneurial sixth sense: how intuition drives stronger decision making." *Medium*, October 5, 2018. https://

medium.com/swlh/entrepreneurial-sixth-sense-how-intu-ition-drives-stronger-decision-making-fc906624641c.

CHAPTER 13

Allen, Summer. "Do Men Have a Gratitude Problem?" *Greater Good Magazine,* August 15, 2018. https://greatergood.berkeley. edu/article/item/do_men_have_a_gratitude_problem.

"COLGATE BRIGHT SMILES, BRIGHT FUTURES®. *Colgate-Pal-molive.* Accessed September 13, 2020. https://www.colgate.com/ en-us/bright-smiles-bright-futures.

"Duchenne smile: A genuine smile that involves the muscles around the eyes." *New Scientist,* accessed September 13, 2020. https:// www.newscientist.com/term/duchenne-smile/.

Emmons, Dr Robert A.. *The Little Book of Gratitude.* London: Octo-pus Books, 2016. https://www.amazon.com/Little-Book-Grat-itude-happiness-wellbeing/dp/1856753654#reader_1856753654.

Kaplan, Janice. "GRATITUDE SURVEY Conducted for the John Templeton Foundation." June-October 2012. Accessed Septem-ber 13, 2020. https://greatergood.berkeley.edu/images/uploads/ JTF_GRATITUDE_REPORTpub.doc.

Kralik, John. *A Simple Act of Gratitude.* New York: Hyperion, 2011.

Laugh for no reason (blog). *Laughter Yoga University.* Accessed Sep-tember 13, 2020. https://laughteryoga.org/laugh-for-no-reason/.

Lee, Janice. "What Humanity Can Learn From Plants: On trees, moss, and feeling at a distance." *Medium.* May 24, 2018. https://medium.com/s/off-beat/what-humanity-can-learn-from-plants-efece7acd3a0.

Matousek, Mark. "The One Life We're Given: A Conversation With Mark Nepo." *Psychology Today,* October 7, 2016. https://www.psychologytoday.com/us/blog/ethical-wisdom/201610/the-one-life-were-given-conversation-mark-nepo.

Mikes, Kimberly. "What Deepak Chopra wants you to know about gratitude." *Happier* (blog), accessed September 24, 2020. https://www.happier.com/blog/what-deepak-chopra-wants-you-to-know-about-gratitude/.

More To That. "Travel Is No Cure for the Mind." *Medium,* March 21, 2018. https://medium.com/personal-growth/travel-is-no-cure-for-the-mind-e449d3109d71.

"Oprah Winfrey Quotes." *Brainy Quote.* Accessed September 24, 2020. https://www.brainyquote.com/quotes/oprah_winfrey_163087.

Robb, Alice. "The Science of Gratitude Says Older Women Are Most Grateful." *The New Republic,* November 27, 2013. https://newrepublic.com/article/115776/science-gratitude.

SoulPancake. "An Experiment in Gratitude | The Science of Happiness." July 11, 2013. Video, 7:13. https://www.youtube.com/watch?v=oHv6vTKD6lg.

Tank, Aytekin. "How gratitude can unlock your leadership potential." *Jotform* (blog), January 3, 2020. https://www.jotform.com/blog/gratitude-leadership/.

TED Talks. "Elizabeth Dunn: Helping others makes us happier—but it matters how we do it." TED2019. Video, 14:21. https://www.ted.com/talks/elizabeth_dunn_helping_others_makes_us_happier_but_it_matters_how_we_do_it.

TEDx Talks. "Laugh. breathe. innovate. | Sushil Bhatia | TEDxYouth@CCHS." October 21, 2018. Video, 18:08. https://www.youtube.com/watch?v=lQMlH5RCfXE.

"The power of gratitude in the workplace." *Science News.* Accessed September 13, 2020. https://www.sciencedaily.com/releases/2019/03/190313091929.htm.

"Thomas A. Edison Quotes." *Brainy Quote.* Accessed September 24, 2020. https://www.brainyquote.com/quotes/thomas_a_edison_132683.

CHAPTER 14

AskNature Team. "Honeybees collaborate when foraging, selecting a new hive through knowledge sharing." *Ask Nature,* August 18, 2016. https://asknature.org/strategy/collaborating-for-group-decisions/.

Brizendine, Louann. *The Female Brain.* New York: Broadway Books, 2006.

Editorial team. "21 Collaboration Statistics that Show the Power of Teamwork." *BIT.AI* (blog). Accessed September 24, 2020. https://blog.bit.ai/collaboration-statistics/.

Gray, Peter. "The play deficit." *Aeon*, accessed September 13, 2020. https://aeon.co/essays/children-today-are-suffering-a-severe-deficit-of-play.

Kenneth Matos. "How fostering collaboration can boost innovation." (blog), *Culture Amp*, accessed September 13, 2020. https://www.cultureamp.com/blog/how-fostering-collaboration-can-boost-innovation/.

Leavitt, Harold J., Jean Lipman-Blumen. "Hot Groups." *HBR,* from the July–August 1995 issue. https://hbr.org/1995/07/hot-groups.

Maawy, Ahmed Mohamed. "The future of disruptive innovation is collaborative." *Medium,* June 2, 2018. https://medium.com/@ahmedmohamedmaawy/the-future-of-disruptive-innovation-is-collaborative-1b9b49b0b107.

Pipes, Taylor. "Lessons in Collaboration & Creativity from Thomas Edison." *Medium,* May 18, 2017. https://medium.com/taking-note/lessons-in-collaboration-creativity-from-thomas-edison-598fcf232fa0.

Shona Project. "Abby Wambach: Be the Wolf." July 5, 2018. Video, 4:59. https://www.youtube.com/watch?v=Fmvg-Myo8WM.

Tank, Aytekin. "A guide to effective (not excessive) collaboration." *Medium,* April 1, 2019. https://medium.com/swlh/a-guide-to-effective-not-excessive-collaboration-cb6c43afb994.

TED Talks. "Margaret Heffernan: Forget the pecking order at work." TEDWomen 2015. Video, 15:39. https://www.ted.com/talks/ margaret_heffernan_forget_the_pecking_order_at_work?language=en.

TED Talks. "Steve Johnson: Where good ideas come from." TED Global 2010. Video, 17:30. https://www.ted.com/talks/steven_ johnson_where_good_ideas_come_from?language=en.

Thorson, Kristen. "Creating a Culture of Collaborative Family Engagement." *Getting Smart,* April 20, 2018. https://www. gettingsmart.com/2018/04/creating-a-culture-of-collabora-tive-family-engagement/.

"Understanding the differences between collaboration and team-work." *Civil Service College.* August, 30, 2018. Accessed September 13, 2020. https://www.civilservicecollege.org. uk/news-understanding-the-differences-between-team-work-and-collaboration-203.

"Vincent Van Gogh Quotes." *Brainy Quote.* Accessed September 24, 2020. https://www.brainyquote.com/quotes/vincent_van_ gogh_120866.

CHAPTER 15

Brow, Robert. "Another Famous Parisian Chef Dumps on Michelin." *Michelin Scars,* June 14, 2019. https://michelinscars. com/2019/06/14/another-famous-parisian-chef-dumps-on-mi-chelin/.

Caulcutt, Clea. "Paris chefs call for end to French kitchen violence." *BBC News*, November 9, 2014. https://www.bbc.com/news/world-europe-30099533.

"Cyril Lignac balances on the contempt of other chefs after his television debut." *PressFrom,* February 28, 2020. https://pressfrom.info/news/politics/-415379-cyril-lignac-balances-on-the-contempt-of-other-chefs-after-his-television-debut.html.

Quotidien avec Yan Barthes. "Invité : Cyril Lignac se raconte dans "Histoires de goûts." March 6, 2020. Video. 19:00. https://www.tf1.fr/tmc/quotidien-avec-yann-barthes/videos/invite-cyril-lignac-se-raconte-dans-histoires-de-gouts-48253701.html.

Labbas, Assia. "France's New Michelin Guide: More Fraternité Than Égalité." *The New York Times,* February 23, 2018. https://www.nytimes.com/2018/02/23/world/europe/michelin-guide-france-women-chefs.html.

Morgan, Zara. "Why are our professional kitchens still male dominated?" *BBC News,* September 16, 2018. https://www.bbc.com/news/uk-wales-45486646.

Theoucafe. "Cyril Lignac—Intégrale du 14/10/2017—Thé ou Café." October 15, 2017. Video, 39:53. https://www.youtube.com/watch?v=xkwA1bAu388.

Walkinshaw, Laura. "The Rise of the Female Michelin Star Chef." *Elite Traveler,* March 6, 2014. https://www.elitetraveler.com/features/the-rise-of-the-female-michelin-star-chef.

CONCLUSION

TEDxSanJuanIsland. "Andrew Bennett: Practical Magic." June 2019. Video, 19:03. https://www.ted.com/talks/andrew_bennett_practical_magic.